There was a Crooked Man

Jason Vail

There was a Crooked Man

THE RICHEST MAN IN TOWN

Copyright 2024, by Jason Vail

Cover design by Ashley Barber. Cover art from istockphoto.com

ISBN: 9798882510007

Hawk Publishing
Tallahassee, FL

Martial Arts

Medieval and Renaissance Dagger Combat

There was a Crooked Man

There was a Crooked Man

March 1265

There was a Crooked Man

Chapter 1

It was a gray March day and One-eye Dick felt bitter, although not about the weather.

"It's unfair, it is," Dick muttered to no one in particular.

One of the wardens at Galdeford Gate, Old Rick, looked out of the shelter of his doorway within the gate passage. "What you say there, Dick?"

"Nuthin'," Dick said. He removed the frayed strand of rag covering his missing eye — the feature that gave him his name — and scratched within the socket. He normally did not remove the rag unless a passer-by was willing to part with greater charity than he or she might be accustomed to in exchange for the opportunity to gaze at his deformity. But even though all traffic leaving Ludlow for points east, like Worcester, Oxford and London, passed through this gate, there hadn't been a single traveler come through all morning to tempt with this display, apart from farmers and woodcutters bringing in supplies, and they always treated Dick as if he was a dead tree or old fence post. In more peaceful times, there had been a lot of traffic. But the war between the king and the rebellious barons under Simon de Montfort and the disorder and crime in the countryside they brought affected the poorest people of Ludlow more harshly than others because they had so little in the first place.

"It's just damned unfair," he said again. It was unfair in Dick's rather slow mind because he had put in a bid for a license to beg at Broad Gate which he reckoned was a better and more lucrative spot, but he had been refused in favor of someone with less seniority on the beggars' list. He had only the slenderest idea that his predicament arose from great forces beyond his vision.

Just then Stephen Attebrook, the tall black-haired deputy sheriff and hundred coroner, limped through the door leading to the undersheriff's office in one of the gate's towers. As often happened, Attebrook favored his bad left foot, which gossip swore had been partly lopped off in a battle against heathens. He had a rolled up parchment thrust through his

9

belt; it was an odd thing to see a man walking about carrying a parchment like that.

Dick momentarily wondered what that parchment might be about, but he had weightier matters to attend to. He held out his bowl, waggling it for emphasis. "How's that pretty wife of yours doing, yer honor?" he said as ingratiatingly as he could manage. His grating voice, which sounded like a rusty hinge, did nothing to help the credibility of his appeal, but he was unaware of this.

Attebrook paused. "You'll bleed me dry, Dick."

"Ah, a great lord like you can afford it," Dick said with a smile which disclosed several missing teeth, one of which had just fallen out a week ago. It was insincere flattery to characterize Attebrook as a great lord; he was only a minor one, with a claim to a single manor.

Attebrook scowled as if he was the victim of a shakedown. But he flipped a halfpenny in Dick's direction. "That's it for the month, hear? And don't spend it all on drink. Get yourself a proper meal. You look terrible."

Dick was, in fact, skinnier than usual. It was a hard winter. He wasn't making much because of the decline of business traffic to a sporadic dribble. He had thought the pickings might be easier at Broad Gate which is why he had bid for a spot there. First, the road from there passed into Mortimer country where there was more order and hence more traffic, and second, his old friend and former beggar, Harry, had done very well there — people said he had saved up enough money to buy himself into the carving business. But Dick knew better. Harry got where he was only because of his unlikely friendship with Attebrook. It was better to have friends and luck than talent and industry. Dick's life was a testament to this principle. He regarded himself as a talented man but his luck had run against him, and he had no friends among the powerful or wealthy.

He snagged the halfpenny and bobbed his head in thanks as Attebrook turned down Tower Street toward the Beast

Market, the intersection of Tower, High, Old and Corve Streets.

"Get yerself something to eat, he says," Dick said morosely. "And where would I do that, eh?" Dick, owing to the fact he never bathed (he regarded it as a waste of time, effort and water) and smelled like a dead horse, wasn't welcome in most taverns or inns of the town, even those that sold fare through open front windows. For a time, he had been tolerated at a tavern in Galdeford, but that ceased after an unfortunate incident of excessive drinking and vomiting. So normally, he had to wait until the end of the day, when he got a morsel at his rooming house on Corve Street.

But a halfpenny was quite a bit of money. He could get half a gallon of ale for it and ale was his first priority. Food came second, although he could buy a whole roast chicken or a half dozen boiled eggs for the same amount.

The nearest place where the proprietor would consider serving him ran a tavern called the Blue Duck at the top of Old Street just outside the Beast Market. Red John Griffin, the proprietor, wouldn't let him inside, but could be cajoled to send up a pitcher if Dick called from the door. Red John was one of those unusual people who was robustly charitable, which was one of the reasons he had failed at every business he had tried so far.

"Hold the fort!" Dick called to Old Rick and tottered down Tower Street, mindful to employ his staff to keep up appearances; he didn't really need it but felt it made him look even more pitiful that he was, which he expected to increase his tips. He wasn't sure it worked but he persevered nonetheless.

The Blue Duck was in the first house on Old Street, down a flight of stairs to the cellar. It was a bit early for the Duck to be open, since it was the end of the dinner hour, but Red John slept in the tavern and might be persuaded to part with some ale if he was home.

Dick descended the first set of stairs to the Duck's door. He rapped on the door and waited. No one answered, so he rapped some more and waited again. Still no response. So after the third iteration of the ritual, he tried the door latch. It lifted and the door opened. He gazed down a second set of stone steps into the depths of the cellar. He saw his own silhouette cast down the stairs and in the rectangle of light at the bottom he saw something else that made him draw a breath. A pair of legs were visible, the rest of the body in darkness. They belonged to Red John.

"Red John!" he called out. "You alright?"

Getting no response, Dick hesitated and then went down the stairs. As he did so, all of Red John became visible in the gloom.

Red John was lying on his stomach. His head was queerly twisted about so that Dick could see his face. He did not look asleep. It looked like he had fallen down the steps.

Dick knelt and shook Red John's shoulder. He felt stiff and solid.

Dick knew about such things. It meant Red John was dead.

That was a disappointment. It meant no ale for Dick … although …

Dick groped his way to the bar that protected the ale kegs from the attentions of the clientele. He found a cup and turned the spigot on one of the barrels to fill the cup. He did this several times, spilling a good bit on himself in his haste to drink as much as he could before discovery.

Someone passed by the doorway above and Dick sensed this was a good time to stop.

He was about to step over the body when another thought occurred to him. He bent down and fumbled in Red John's belt pouch for his purse; it was on his right hip so, mercifully, Dick didn't have to turn him over. As Dick hoped, it held a few coins. He poured them into his palm and replaced the purse. Thus invigorated by ale and additional funds, he climbed back to the street.

As Dick mounted the last of the steps, he came face to face with Harry Carver. Harry had lost his legs some years ago and had propelled himself about with his hands and powerful arms. But since becoming a carver, he had acquired a fancy little cart pulled by a fancy little pony that he used to get about town. The sight of Harry now, in the bloom of his success, provoked spasms of jealousy and it was no different at this moment.

"Afternoon, Dick," Harry said pleasantly as he stopped the cart to avoid having his pony collide with Dick.

"Afternoon," Dick said shortly.

Before Dick could scurry away, Harry spotted the open door to the Duck, which Dick had neglected to close. That door should not be standing open like that.

"What you up to?" Harry asked.

"Me? Nothing. I, er, I — something's happened to Red John!" Dick blurted out. He hadn't wanted to say anything, but once someone else discovered Red John, Harry would remember running into Dick outside the Duck. With the door open. Suspicions would be raised.

"What do you mean, something's happened to Red John?" Harry asked.

"I-I think he's dead," Dick said.

"Dead?" Harry asked as if he did not believe what he had heard.

Harry swung himself to the ground with grace astonishing to those unfamiliar with him. He paused at the head of the stairs. Harry did not like stairs. They were a major obstacle. Getting up and down required considerable effort, especially the part about going up. He looked at Dick — not that he could expect any help from that quarter — and then let himself down as far as the door. He peered in.

"I see what you mean," Harry said.

He pulled himself back up to the street and then climbed into the cart.

There must have been something about Dick's expression that still bothered Harry.

"Is this like last time?" Harry asked in an accusatory tone.

"Last time?" Dick stammered. "I don't know what you mean."

"You sure do. I mean that business with the ring."

Dick wanted to curse Harry for his quick wittedness. He was altogether too clever for his own or anyone else's good. The reference to the ring was to an unfortunate incident last autumn when Dick accidentally discovered the skeletal remains of two men on the road north of Onibury. He had also found a bejeweled ring among the bones, which he fetched away to his profit, although that had caused both him and others a great deal of trouble.

Dick shuffled his feet.

Harry held out a hand. "Give it over, whatever you've got."

Dick surrendered the pennies he pilfered from Red John's purse, retaining only the halfpenny. "Sir Steve gave me this one," he said. "Ask him about it when you get the chance."

"I will," Harry said, slipping the pennies in his pouch.

"You won't say anything about this, will you?" Dick asked.

"It never happened. Looks like you're the first finder. You better wait here," Harry said. "I'll fetch Sir Stephen."

Chapter 2

Stephen Attebrook spread the parchment on the parapet of Ludlow Castle's west wall. He held it in place against a light breeze but didn't read it. His eyes and his thoughts were on the River Teme directly below, Whitcliffe just across the river and, most importantly, the wide farmland to the north of a long, forested ridge that ran westward. That farmland was his, the manor of Halton Priors.

He would much rather be there than here. His manor and his family needed all his attention. The manor had been sacked and burned last summer by a force supporting the barons under his deadly enemy Nigel FitzSimmons, and was only now on the verge of recovering from the terrific shock. His family and his village's people had got through the winter only by dint of significant belt tightening, meaning people ate less to conserve what little they had been able to harvest from a damaged crop and from the animals that had escaped the raiders, so they went hungry to bed and got up in the morning to face a daunting day of labor with aching stomachs. February was always a hard month for everyone, when the last stocks began to run out, but that had been especially true at Halton Priors. Everyone prayed that this coming year would be better than the last.

On the good side, the task of rebuilding burnt homes had gone ahead quite well, since peasant homes were easy to throw up as they consisted only of a few timber supports, wattle-and-daub walls and piles of thatch for the roofs. All that was necessary was the materials, which were cut down from Stephen's forest, and the labor, which was not in short supply over winter. So everyone had as warm a place to sleep as could be hoped for.

That left the question of the manor house. It was a burned-out stone shell, reeking of the stench of charred wood even after so many months. It would take every penny Stephen could save to rebuild it. Having a new and proper stone house was Ida's dream. For the present, though, she had to make do with a simple timber thing that had been thrown up for the Attebrooks' use when they spent nights at the manor. Now that his young wife was pregnant, Stephen felt even more pressure to see that project through, but it would probably take years.

Yet duty, and the coming resumption of the war between the forces loyal to the king and those supporting Earl Simon de Montfort, required Stephen to be here, stuck in the castle. It had fallen to Montfort last summer, but then Stephen led a force that had retaken it in December at the behest of Baron Roger Mortimer, one of the king's staunchest partisans. Stephen thought he had got off the hook of duty after the recapture of the castle, but Mortimer thought otherwise. He required Stephen to assume the post of deputy constable, which meant that he had to spend most of his time here, when he wasn't pursuing his duties as hundred coroner and deputy sheriff of Shropshire. Fortunately, there had not been much call for a coroner or a deputy sheriff over winter.

But that had changed.

His eyes fell at last to the letter. It was from James de Alditheley, the sheriff jointly of Shropshire and Staffordshire.

> *To Sir Stephen Attebrook from Sir James de Alditheley, greetings —*
>
> *I request and require that you attend to the following urgent business soonest. I have received numerous complaints about rapine and pillage occurring in the southeastern part of Shropshire, southwest Staffordshire. These appear to be coordinated attacks by the same person or persons unknown, and the depredations have become so widespread over the winter and the complaints so manifold that I cannot ignore them any longer. Enquiries have been made about who might be behind these outrages, but so far none have made any headway on that score, other than the suspicion that they are the work of a single gang of cutthroats. Your talent for finding answers to the inscrutable has come to my mind, so I require that you bend your considerable talents to the identification of this nest of bandits as soon as possible. I will place at your disposal a force*

of five men to assist in your investigation. This letter will serve as your warrant and appointment as deputy for Staffordshire as well as Shropshire. Please advise by return post that you will give this matter your full and immediate attention.

Stephen read the letter through twice, feeling glum. It would mean riding about swathes of two counties, and perhaps sleeping rough a lot of the time. He might be away from home for months on this business, and in all likelihood he would find nothing useful. Robbers were often as elusive as smoke.

But there was nothing he could do but obey. He had committed homicide last autumn — not the first time, but the first time he had been caught at it. Even though the killings were in self-defense, the law still required that he obtain a royal pardon. With Montfort in power, there was no chance that a pardon would be his, since like it or not he was a king's man. Alditheley had refrained from arresting him on the implied promise that he serve as a deputy sheriff. With that appointment had come some degree of immunity from arrest for his participation in the retaking of Ludlow Castle. The bill had now come due in earnest.

He folded the parchment and stuffed it in his belt pouch, to keep it safe from the weather, since he would need it again if anyone in Staffordshire challenged his right to act there. He turned to face the castle's cramped inner bailey.

Harry Carver was just driving his little cart through the gate tower. Harry waved at him. Stephen raised a hand in return.

"Hey, Stephen!" Harry called. "You're needed! There's been a death!"

"Of course, there has," Stephen muttered. What was it they said about trouble: it always came in buckets? He called back, "I'll be right down!"

Stephen and Gilbert Wistwode stared down the stairs of the Blue Duck.

"You touched nothing?" Stephen asked One-eye Dick.

"No, sir, I never," Dick said.

Stephen knew this to be a lie. Harry had told him about Dick rifling the contents of Red John's purse. But he wasn't going to make an issue of it since Harry had forced him to surrender what he had taken. "You touched him, though."

"To make sure he was dead, yessir," Dick said.

"Turned him over?"

"No, sir. Red John's as hard as a block of wood."

Stephen nodded. If Dick had committed any more mischief than pilfering the purse, it was unlikely he would admit to it.

"I suppose we should get this over with," he said to Gilbert.

"The sooner the better," the round little clerk sighed. His round, usually jovial face was sad. "Poor Red John. Bad luck followed him around like Dick's bad smell."

"Hey," Dick said. "You've no call talking about me like that."

"He's just making an observation," Harry said. "There's privies with better smells than you, Dick."

Stephen glanced around one last time. Just to the rear was the wide expanse of the Beast Market. It was a busy place as usual, with carts and wagons and people on foot going this way and that. A trio of women carrying wicker baskets came past them from the market to head down Old Street. Stephen recognized two of them as stocking makers whose shop was by Brand Lane. They nodded to him in recognition and he nodded back, then they put their heads together and excited whispers could be heard. As yet, no crowd had gathered as usually happened with deaths in this town. But that must mean no one had heard about Red John's sad tumble down the stairs. With Stephen and Gilbert conferring on the street, however, it was likely that tongues would wag and the usual mob would collect for what entertainment it could squeeze out of someone else's misfortune.

Stephen was two steps down the stairs when Harry said, "Say, Stephen, you wouldn't mind giving me a hand, would you? You know how I hate stairways."

"There's no reason for you to come down," Stephen said.

"Well, someone's got to watch the door," Harry said. "You know, to keep people out so you won't be bothered."

This was not Harry's real reason. He could guard the door just as well from the street, but he wanted to see and hear what happened below so he could report it when he got back to his shop. Although his carving business was flourishing, he reckoned that it helped if people dropped by for the latest news, meanwhile being tempted by sweet talk into buying what he had on sale. Everybody could use more cut-price spoons, cups or wooden bowls.

"All right," Stephen said resignedly, not wishing to interfere with commerce. He turned his back to take Harry upon it, grunting with strain at the sudden weight, for Harry was all hard muscle with a massive chest, shoulders and arms.

He managed to make it down to the doorway without falling, although he staggered twice, and he was able to deposit Harry at the threshold without killing either of them.

The distance was not far, but the strain left Stephen panting, and he paused to recover his breath. "You first," he said to Gilbert.

"My pleasure," Gilbert said, although there was nothing pleasurable about what they had to do. It was Stephen's job as hundred coroner to mount an inquiry into suspicious deaths, which meant he was called out for every random accident, since the crown regarded these as suspicious as any murder and required the hundred to pay a fine on the instrument that caused the death. Because the people of the hundred were taxed to pay these fines, there was a strong incentive to keep them as small as possible. In Stephen's tenure, he had been forced to fine stones on which a woman had tripped and fatally knocked her head; a horseshoe that had come loose resulting in a fall that killed a gentry man (the jury had deadlocked over whether to blame the loose nail or the entire shoe; there was never any question of the horse being at fault); the loose rung of a ladder; a candle which had caused a deadly fire; and many more small innocuous things that had taken someone's life. Gilbert, as Stephen's clerk and friend, accompanied him on every inquiry, although strictly speaking he did not have to.

It was dark within the cellar when Stephen reached the dirt floor where Red John's body lay at the foot of the steep stone stairway. He looked up at the doorway above his head, which provided the only illumination, and measured those stairs. He agreed with Dick's speculation that Red John had fallen; such a fall could easily be deadly. He imagined poor Red John slipping or tripping and pitching forward to land on his head. Stephen shuddered at the thought. What a sad, terrible, useless way to die.

"This shouldn't take long," Stephen said, turning to the body.

The body was that of a slender man, almost as tall as Stephen, who looked down upon others from six feet of height. John Griffin was known about Ludlow as Red John to distinguish him from the dozens of other Johns hereabout owing to his bright red hair. On closer examination and despite the dim light, Stephen could see streaks of gray among the red, even though Red John's face looking over his right shoulder in an unnatural way was unlined and did not look his age, which was about ten years older than Stephen; that is, in his late thirties. One of his eyes was half open, the other closed.

Stephen felt the dead man's face. The flesh was rigid. The way his head was turned around it was clear he died of a broken neck.

"He died sometime last night, don't you think?" Stephen said.

"A good enough working assumption," Gilbert said.

"For now," Stephen said with a slight smile.

"For now," Gilbert agreed.

It was nearing the time that most taverns opened up, yet none of Red John's servants had shown up.

"Harry!" Stephen called. "Do you know who works here?"

"Besides Red John?" Harry said. "No one. He ran the place himself."

"Alone?" Stephen said, surprised. "With no help?"

"Well, I heard he had a girl working here, but she quit when he couldn't pay her wages," Harry said.

"Did he still owe her money?" The question came involuntarily to Stephen's lips, prompted by a mind tuned to sense suspicious things; not that there seemed to be anything suspicious about this death.

"As far as I know. She was pretty bitter about it. Not that I blame her."

"How long ago was that?"

"I don't know. Weeks, months."

That seemed to rule out the terminated servant. It was unlikely that she, or more likely a husband or father, would take weeks or months to work themselves up to revenge. Stephen snorted. "You're supposed to be the font of all gossip, Harry. And yet you fail me."

"I only repeat what I know. I never make stuff up, like some people."

"What else do you know about him?"

"A bit. He was the fourth or fifth son of some lord in Worcestershire, or was it Staffordshire? I never cared enough about that to clarify the point. His father set him up as a draper but Red John made a mess of things. The business failed and he sold what was left of his stock to that fellow Baynard. He tried his hand at cattle dealing, but never made a go of that either. He complained to me once when I was at Broad Gate about how his family wouldn't lift a finger to help, said he had to sink or swim on his own. I guess he used what little money he had left to set himself up as a tavernkeeper, but he wasn't doing well at that either. As you can see from the sad state of this place."

Except for the record of failure, it was not an unusual tale. If a younger son did not go into the church, make a good marriage with an heiress, or attach himself to the house of a wealthy and powerful man, the lesser gentry often established the unlucky son in the town as a merchant. Stephen's own father had done something similar by arranging for him to become a clerk to a royal justice in hopes he would someday become a lawyer. That had not worked out.

"He never married," Gilbert said.

"You knew him as well?" Stephen asked.

"Passingly. We are rather in the same business." Gilbert and his wife Edith owned the Broken Shield Inn across the street from Stephen's townhouse.

"No family, then," Stephen said.

"No one in town, anyway," Harry said.

That meant there was no family to take care of the body.

Stephen's usual practice was to cut the clothes from a body when there was some doubt about the manner of death — by failing to make a thorough examination he had once mistaken a stabbing for a drowning, and he so smarted from that humiliation that he was unwilling to risk another. Even after years had faded everyone else's memory of the matter he still felt the sting.

But usually, there had been family to ensure that the dead were reverently shrouded and buried. Here if Stephen followed his customary practice Red John's nakedness would be exposed to strangers, and without any family nearby, who would care for the body when they were done?

However, the manner of death seemed obvious. So instead of pulling out his knife, he drew up Red John's coat and linen shirt to see his back. It was smooth and white, unmarked and unbruised. There were no wounds.

He had Gilbert help him flip over the corpse so he could conduct the same examination of Red John's chest and stomach, obtaining the same result apart from the purplish skin. Nothing remarkable there, except that Red John's ribs were unduly prominent.

"Hasn't been eating well," Gilbert summed things up.

"Doesn't look like it," Stephen said. "It's odd, though."

"What's odd?" Gilbert asked.

"If he fell down the stairs don't you think you'd see marks on his back or front?"

"Perhaps he fell on one of the last steps," Gilbert said cautiously. "And went headfirst into the ground. *Crack!* And he was a dead man."

"Maybe. But if he had done so the body would be closer to the bottom step if not partly on it, don't you think? Look, his feet are at least a foot away."

"Hmm, I see what you mean."

Next Stephen examined Red John's hands. Like the rest of him, they were slender with long delicate fingers. The nails were well trimmed. Although they were red and chapped from what probably was strong soap — indicating he did his own washing — they bore no signs of violence. People who fell down stairs often dislocated or broke fingers throwing out their hands to save themselves. But there was none of that here.

Stephen turned his attention to Red John's head. He ran his fingers through that mop of red hair, probing for injuries to the skull and peering closely for any cuts. Nothing.

He rocked back on his heels. "We'll have to cut off his coat and shirt after all."

"Very well," Gilbert said without enthusiasm. More often than not, this unwholesome chore fell to him.

"On second thought, perhaps we only need to do the arms, I think."

"That's a relief."

"You take the left one, I'll do the right."

"My, you are gracious this time."

"Noblesse oblige, I always say."

"Well, thank you, my lord."

"Think nothing of it."

They sawed away with their knives. As they worked there were flickers of light in the doorway and the murmur of voices above.

Harry said, "You can't go in there" to someone out of sight.

"Why not?" an indignant male voice protested, moving into view to loom over Harry.

"The coroner's down there," Harry said. "He's not to be disturbed."

"What's going on?"

"There's been an accident."

"What sort of accident?"

"A bad one, you idiot. What do you imagine?"

"Ah, right, if Attebrook's here. Is it Red John? Can we see?"

"No," Harry said firmly. "Stay back."

"You're in no position to tell us what to do."

"I am, if you don't want a tumble down those things yourself."

"You're getting entirely too big for yourself if you think you can order us around."

"I may be short now, but I'm a bigger man than you," Harry said.

"Harry!" Stephen shouted. "Is there a problem? Do I need to come up?"

"Is there a problem?" Harry asked the silhouettes above him.

"I don't suppose there is," the voice grumbled, finally appreciating that Harry was doing Stephen's bidding. "Is it Red John?"

"Yeah," Harry said.

"Fell down the stairs, you think?"

"Looks like it."

"Hey!" the voice called out. "Red John's dead!" which prompted other voices to call out the news and Stephen heard it passing down Old Street and into the Beast Market. A crowd gathered on the street outside the Blue Duck.

"So much for solitary labor," Stephen said as he removed one of Red John's sleeves.

"At least we're almost done," Gilbert said, finishing his part.

There were no marks either on Red John's arms that might have happened in a roll down the stairs.

"What do you think?" Gilbert asked.

"He broke his neck somehow."

"Or had it broken for him, then?"

"I'm beginning to think so. With the body so far from the stairs I don't see how he could have ended up here if it was a fall."

Gilbert shook his head. "Who'd want to kill Red John? He was such a pleasant fellow. Everybody liked him."

"That doesn't make him immune from robbery or a jealous husband."

"Red John wasn't the sort of person to diddle someone's wife. He didn't take much interest in women."

"Temptation can wear down even the most iron resolve," Stephen said. "You more than anyone should know about that."

Indeed, Gilbert had once been a monk at Greater Wenlock Priory living a life of chastity and contemplation until he had succumbed to his wife Edith's charms.

"Let's not talk about it," Gibert said, embarrassed.

Done with the examination of the body, Stephen now had the opportunity to survey the cellar. There were three tables with benches, one of which was missing a leg; an invitation to further accident and mayhem. On one of the tables there was a pitcher and three wooden cups, and a fourth cup lay on the ground. A candle burned down to a nub stood by the pitcher. Stephen checked the contents of the cups; they were empty, but the pitcher was half filled with wine. That seemed unusual. A cheap tavern like this rarely served wine. The floor was hard-packed dirt. There was a rickety bar that looked as though it might topple at any moment whose purpose was to protect the half dozen small kegs on a table from unauthorized sampling by the guests. The kegs were the sixteen-gallon kind called kilderkins. With the door shut, illumination would be by weak tallow lamps, one to a table, that gave off only enough light to keep people from stumbling over things on the floor. Even now, Stephen could smell the residual stench of those cheap lamps. It was, as Harry said, a sad place where drinks could be had cheap. But then even Ludlow's poorest deserved a place for diversion.

He tapped the tabletop with his fingers while he looked about some more. In a far corner, there was a straw pallet with a rumpled blanket on top.

"He slept here?" Stephen asked.

"Yeah," Harry answered. "He had a chamber above but he lost it. Couldn't meet the rent."

"What did Dick say about how he got in?" Stephen asked.

"He said he just opened the door," Harry said.

"It wasn't barred, then," Stephen said to himself, for he now saw a five-foot length of board leaning by the door which had to be its bar.

"Ah, ha!" Gilbert said. "He closed up for the night and went to bed. Sometime after dark he had visitors, three in number. He let them in. They shared a drink and then his visitors snapped his neck."

"That seems to be the size of it," Stephen said.

"A sad end for a decent man," Harry said.

They had been overheard, of course, and shouts transmitted this conclusion to the crowd outside. It wouldn't be long before everyone in Ludlow knew about it.

Chapter 3

The crowd on the street began to break up and drift away now that everyone knew it was murder and how it was done. Besides, people had work to do and couldn't afford to fritter away the day.

Meanwhile, the housewife for the family living above brought down a linen sheet. "Poor man," she sighed as she helped Gilbert spread it over the body. "He was such a nice man to my children — always ready to buy them a sweetmeat in the market."

"And yet you kicked him out of your house when he couldn't make the rent," Harry observed from the top of the stairs.

The woman shot Harry a venomous glance, and she said, "I need the rent. I've four children to feed and no husband to provide for us."

"You'll be leaving the sheet?" Stephen asked.

"Well, I do expect to be paid for it," the woman said, and beat a quick retreat, swerving around Harry and disappearing.

"You'll need to contact the priest," Stephen said, referring to the priest presiding at the parish church of Saint Lawrence. "He'll have to see after Griffin's burial."

"He'll want payment," Gilbert said, for burial in the churchyard required payment of a fee. Otherwise, it would be the paupers' ground on Upper Galdeford Road.

"Yes," Stephen said, remembering something he had forgotten to look for — Red John's money box.

"I'll see the priest," Gilbert said, and climbed the stairs to the street.

Stephen saw nothing that could be such a box behind the bar or anywhere else in the cellar, which was bare except for the pallet, kegs and tables, and had begun poking about Red John's sleeping pallet when, one by one, the coroner's jurors for Ludlow appeared. Stephen showed them the body, explained what he had found and gave his conclusions. None of them wanted to dispute him, so Stephen gave assignments requiring several jurors to question the neighbors about whether they had seen or heard anything.

Going back to the pallet, he threw it aside in exasperation, having found nothing. He was sure it would be here, since there was nowhere else in this barren place to conceal a money box or even a purse. He was about to give up when it came to him that Red John probably had done the same thing with his savings that Stephen did with his: buried it. The most likely place was under the pallet, so he got down on hands and knees and probed the ground with his dagger. Sure enough, after a short time, the dagger struck something in the corner that didn't feel like a stone. Stephen scraped aside a few inches of dirt and came upon a buried box. He carried it into the light at the foot of the stairs, where he lifted the latch and then the lid.

"How much is there?" Harry asked.

Stephen stirred the collection of pennies with a forefinger. "Looks like about a shilling. From what you said about him, I'm surprised there's that much. Enough to buy him a decent burial, I would think."

"That is unusual. Red John wasn't much for saving money," Harry said. "But the main thing is that the money's there."

"Right," Stephen said. "This probably wasn't a robbery gone bad." He glanced at the body now concealed by the sheet. "What if he quarreled with his visitors?"

"He wasn't the quarrelsome type."

"Deliberate murder, then," Stephen said.

"You think somebody had it in for Red John? The man didn't have an enemy in the world. Everybody liked him."

"Did he owe anyone money apart from that servant? Someone who might have wanted the debt collected?" Now that this seemed like murder, Stephen had to consider the possibility more seriously that it was over an unpaid debt; money, jealousy and pride were the main reasons people killed each other.

Harry shrugged. "He always owed people. Doesn't look like Thumper's work, though."

Thumper meant Will Thumper, a notorious local criminal who specialized in the sale of stolen goods, although he doubled as a debt collector.

"Yes," Stephen sighed. Thumper was known to treat his targets roughly but he had never, as far as anyone knew, killed one of them. It was easier to get money from damaged but living debtors than from dead ones.

He glanced at the gray sky behind Harry. He was about to say, "What's got into Gilbert?" because he was impatient to be away from this dreadful place, but the sight of another figure coming down to Harry and blocking the light from the doorway stayed his tongue.

"What's going on here?" the newcomer exclaimed at the threshold.

"A spot of murder," Harry said. "Surely you've heard about it."

"Murder?" the newcomer said, shocked. He pointed a finger at the shrouded figure on the cellar floor. "That can't be …" His voice trailed off.

"Red John Griffin," Stephen said.

"Somebody wringed his neck," Harry added. He made twisting motions with his hands, the sort people used to break a chicken's neck.

"Oh, no!" the new man cried. He rushed down the steps and knelt by the corpse's side. He reached for the sheet to pull it aside, but Stephen grasped his wrists.

"Who are you?" Stephen demanded.

"I am Ralph le Dyne, steward of Fox Hall," he said. He was a man in his fifties with gray hair and beard. The reference to Fox Hall meant nothing to Stephen.

"You knew Red John?"

"Of course, I knew him," Dyne said heavily. "I've just come from Fox Hall. His brother was murdered in the Wyre Forest on Saturday. I came to tell him that he is the heir. Or was."

At this, Stephen saw no reason to deny Dyne a look at the corpse and drew back the sheet for him. Grief shook Dyne and he was incapable of further speech, so Stephen guided him to one of the benches. One remedy for shock was a good drink. Stephen fetched a cup that seemed to be clean from the sideboard, and poured wine from the pitcher on the table. Then he sat down beside Dyne.

"Fox Hall is a manor, I take it," Stephen said.

Dyne drank all his wine in one gulp and set the empty cup on his lap. "In Staffordshire within the Wyre Forest."

"Red John's brother was the lord?"

"William, yes," Dyne said. "I can't believe they're all dead now, all five of them."

Stephen coaxed the story from him. The Griffin family had five sons. The eldest died at seventeen after a fall from a horse. The second was lost at sea on the way to France. The third, William, inherited the manor and was killed in the forest the preceding Saturday. The fourth died of the plague three years ago in London, where he was a wine importer. That left Red John, the youngest, to inherit once William was gone. But now he was dead too.

"A terrible end of a great family," Dyne said. "Such kind and generous people — all of them."

"You said your lord William was killed Saturday. Tell me what you know," Stephen said.

"He went to Bewdley on that morning with a single groom," Dyne said. "I've warned him time and again that it wasn't safe. There have been so many robberies on the roads, you see. We've heard terrible tales of ghastly murders on the roads thereabout. People butchered in the most horrible way. But he dismissed my warning. It was such a short way to Bewdley. Nothing untoward was likely to happen, he said, although I vigorously disagreed. But the man was smitten. Love addled his judgment."

"How so?"

"He was infatuated with a young woman in Bewdley. A certain Ingrede Paddoc. Her father is a riverman. He has a business carrying goods up the Severn from Gloucester. Ingrede, I must admit, is a most beautiful young woman. Many have sought her hand or her attentions, even those of the gentry like Lord William. I've always thought her a canny lass, looking out for her best interests in terms of a match. She had many suitors, including Richard de Plumton, a rich and influential fellow, and played them off one against the other. I thought she would settle on Plumton, but she surprised me and accepted Lord William's proposal of marriage. A most unsuitable marriage, if you ask me, but I had nothing to say about it.

"But we are off track. You wanted to know about William's death," Dyne went on. "Both horses came back with empty saddles late in the day. One of the saddles had blood on it. I immediately rode out to see what happened. The bodies were about two miles from the manor. Both had been cut to pieces — just as we have heard has happened to others." He shivered. "I never expected such evil to strike so close to home."

Stephen nodded toward Red John's corpse. "Has he any family left?"

"Only a handful of cousins."

"Can they be counted on to take charge of the body and see that it gets a descent burial?"

"I doubt it," Dyne said. "They were not close, any of the cousins. Well, perhaps except for one. But he is too far away to involve in this business."

"What about you? Can you take care of him?"

"I will be glad to do John this last service."

"What will you do with him? I've sent my clerk to the church to see about burial there."

"I'll take him back to the manor. He can lie with his parents and brothers. That is most fitting."

"I will leave it to you then," Stephen said.

"Yes," Dyne said. To the room at large he added in a wan voice, "I shall have to find a wagon somewhere."

Stephen pointed down Old Street. "There's a carter who lives on the other side of the gate. His name is Godric. A young fellow, but reliable. You might check there to see if he's available for hire."

"I will, thank you."

"When do you propose to leave?" Stephen asked.

"As soon as possible. Tomorrow, if that can be done."

"I will go with you."

"I appreciate your offer of escort, but I'm sure I can find a traveling party heading my way."

"I'll come just the same."

Dyne climbed the stairs and eased around Harry. Stephen followed, closing the door behind him, only now noticing the chain and padlock on the step by the door; Red John must have used that to lock up when he was out. He squatted to allow Harry to mount his back, suppressing a gasp at Harry's weight, even though it was expected. And then he laboriously clawed upward to the street.

Harry had to go on his way when they reached the street. A man of business could tarry only so long over such an amusement as murder before life demanded the attention it was due, and he had carved bedsteads to deliver.

Stephen waited at the top of the stairs, fending off questions from curious passers-by with iron stares until Gilbert finally arrived with Father Bartholomew, one of the priests at Saint Lawrence's Church, and two church boys pulling a handcart. Father Bartholomew was relieved that there would be no demand for space in the churchyard, which had grown so crowded that new burials took place upon old ones. You could barely turn a spadeful of dirt without disturbing the bones of the previously departed and largely forgotten.

Meanwhile, the two jurors who had volunteered to question the neighbors came back. Phillip Sibbetone, a glover whose shop was on Upper Corve Street, said they'd learned nothing; nobody saw or heard anything.

"No raised voices?" Stephen waved an exasperated hand at the house that stood over the tavern in the cellar. "No argument?"

"Not a peep," said the bottle maker William Brandone. "Quiet as a church on Tuesday."

"Can we go now?" Sibbetone said. He disliked spending any more time on coroner business than he had to.

"Be off then," Stephen sighed and waved them away. They departed and left Stephen to stew in a growing sense of hopelessness. There was no evidence pointing to a perpetrator, no witness, no articles left at the scene that might be associated with the killer, nothing that he could rely on to make an accusation and an arrest. People had little patience with the fact that many crimes defied solution. The townspeople expected answers and would hold Stephen responsible if the killer wasn't promptly caught and killed again. And failure always received more celebration than success; there were no doubt many in town and perhaps elsewhere who would be glad to see him fail. Perhaps the only thing to do now was wait and pray that something turned up that would point the way.

There were, however, other matters that needed his attention, the sooner the better. Stephen stalked up Old Street to the Beast Market. Gilbert hurried at his heels.

"Have you had a thought?" Gilbert asked as he panted to keep up. "Did you learn something from that steward?"

"Not about Red John," Stephen said as they turned down Tower Street toward Galdeford Gate. He halted and thrust the parchment toward Gilbert.

"Not a bad hand, this fellow," said Gilbert, connoisseur of handwriting, when he finished reading. "You could take a lesson from him. Your script is chicken scratch by comparison. You've had a thought about this, then."

"I wonder if the men who killed William Griffin are those I've been ordered to find," Stephen said.

"Well, the roads are full of bandits," Gilbert said skeptically. "It could have been someone else."

"True. Mustn't leap to conclusions. There will always be robberies. You hang one robber and three more spring up to take his place."

They reached the gate, entered the sheriff's tower and climbed the circular stairs to the first floor, where the undersheriff, Thomas de Hames, maintained his office. Hames was not there, but his clerk, Percy Nelonde, was and he pestered Stephen with questions about the Griffin killing while Stephen laboriously wrote his reply to Sheriff Alditheley, lettering carefully because Gilbert was watching.

"This goes out with the next post," Stephen said, handing over the letter to the clerk, pleased that he had avoided answering questions in a meaningful and informative way. People were too curious about things that they should let lie.

"As you wish, sir," the Nelonde said.

"And the sheriff says I am to have five men to assist me," Stephen said. "Who will those be?"

"I haven't a clue, sir. You'll have to ask the undesheriff. It will be his decision."

"Where is he? I need to get this matter sorted out right away."

"Well, he's, er, gone to Shrewsbury. Won't be back for several days, I expect."

Stephen tapped his thigh impatiently. If there was anything to be done about the murder of William Griffin and that band of robbers, it had to be done right away — the possibility of additional killings was even more acute where there was a known, active gang wreaking havoc about the countryside than in the matter of Red John's death. He didn't think he could afford any delay.

"How many bailiffs does Hames have here now? Eight? They seem to change so often that I can't keep track," Stephen said.

"When they're sober, eight, yessir. At the moment."

"I'll have them all summoned. Now."

"Well, I can't rightly do that. All of them are out in the hundreds collecting the sheriff's farm, and attending to hundred courts, as you know they must, sir." Sheriffs usually held their counties "at farm," which meant they paid a fee to the crown rather like rent and kept what was left over from their exactions for themselves. This was always a tidy sum. Only a lot of money could coerce someone to take on the administration of a county. It was a great deal of work and risky: if a sheriff failed in some duty, he could be fined himself. Yet prudent and careful men could become well off as a result of such an appointment, which made the risk worth the while.

"Pffttt!" Stephen snorted in disgust. So much for the sheriff's support.

Chapter 4

Stephen went home in a foul mood. He tried turning his thoughts elsewhere — despite his initial misgivings, there were things to do about Red John's murder, people to question, like the nights' watch and the wardens of the gates for any unusual comings or goings; someone may have seen or heard something that could make a difference. But these efforts foundered on his frustration at being left to pursue an important inquiry across two counties without any help. God, he wished he could chuck both problems and retire to a comfortable chair by his hearth fire, and ride out on sunny afternoons to his manor of Halton Priors to keep a lordly eye on the spring plowing.

"It was that bad?" Ida asked at Stephen's scowl when he entered the hall.

It took Stephen a moment to realize she meant Red John's murder. She had heard about it, of course. "We've seen much worse. It's more that there seems there's nothing to be done about it. And there's this."

He handed her Alditheley's letter. Ida scanned it quickly.

"Does it mean what I think it means?" she asked.

"I have to go away," Stephen said. "I don't know for how long. I'm sorry. And there won't be any bailiffs to help. Hames has sent them all off so there's none to spare for me."

"Alditheley expects you to catch these bandits by yourself?" she said incredulously.

"No. To be fair, I think it means he just intends me to find out who they are and where they are hiding. When I've done that, Alditheley can mount an expedition against them."

"This does not sound the least bit safe. You, by yourself, against vicious robbers and murderers."

"I'll have Gilbert and Wymar with me."

"Oh, yes, they will make a difference. Well, there's a lot to make ready, then." Ida smoothed her hands on her apron and headed to the pantry.

By nightfall, one end of the long table in the hall was stacked with supplies — blankets, traveling cloaks and coats, a change of underclothes and stockings, the bags containing Stephen's mail, his shield, helmet and sword, his bow and bag of arrows, several large sausages, cheeses, and two loaves of bread, a bag of dried apples. It was a good thing he had two baggage horses to carry all of it.

Stephen eyed the pile with some misgivings. He was used to traveling light. But he said nothing because Ida had gone to a great deal of effort to collect it all; especially the sausages, which she had to beg from Edith Wistwode, proprietress of the Broken Shield Inn across the street. The only thing Ida had forgotten was his archer's clothes, a soiled old hat, a worn coat, a beat-up woolen shirt, and shabby cloak. He might not need them but it was better to have them just in case. He fetched the bag with that stuff and put it in the pile.

The extended family had a light supper, the five adults — Harry and his wife Joan, Harry's sister Sarah, Ida and Stephen — at what was left of the table and the children on the ground, since there was no room for them. Sarah, who was now the housekeeper, had only been with the family since the winter, but she, Joan and Ida had become good friends and they chattered among each other when they had exhausted Harry of his font of knowledge about Red John's murder. Ida intercepted any questions aimed at Stephen so he wasn't forced to talk much; he was never a great conversationalist even in the best of times. He was grateful for this, and his mood had begun to brighten.

As on most evenings, the family retired early. After seeing Christopher, Stephen's young son, tucked on his pallet with the other boys, Stephen and Ida groped in the dark to the stairway after Joan covered the remaining coals of the hearth fire with a big clay pot to prevent sparks from flying out and burning everyone as they slept.

Ida paused at the foot of the stairs, hands at her temples.

"Is something wrong?" Stephen asked.

"I just — I just feel a bit weak and wobbly all of a sudden," she said. Ida had been suffering from morning sickness and hadn't been able to keep much down.

"Well, then. I guess you need some help." Stephen lifted her onto his shoulder, since the stairs were too narrow and steep to allow him to carry her in his arms, and mounted the stairs.

"You oaf," she said when he set her down.

"But a loveable one."

Ida pinched his cheek. "Sometimes. Today you've been a terrible grouch." She took him by the hand and led him into the bed chamber.

Chapter 5

Godric Carter had come up in the world in the last few years, since he had inherited the carting business upon the murder of his father, Patrick Carter, and the disappearance of his older brother, Edgar. He had a new wagon, painted red and blue, and two horses to pull it, indications that he was indeed doing well for himself and his growing family. He and his wife Emily had one child and, according to Harry, there was a second on the way.

Godric was waiting at the door to the Blue Duck with Dyne when Stephen, Gilbert and Stephen's young squire, Wymar, arrived on their horses. They were wrapped in heavy coats and cloaks, for the weather was just above freezing and there was a bitter wind that swept down Old Street, stirring little spirals of dust. The sun had just risen and the street was in shadow.

"Morning, sir," Godric said to Stephen. They were well known to each other. Stephen had investigated the murder of Godric's father, and that murder led his twin brother Edgar to kill the man he responsible. Stephen should have turned Edgar over to the sheriff for prosecution, but in a moment of weakness and sympathy, he had arranged for Edgar to escape. Edgar was living under another name in York, the last Stephen heard, married to a girl named Pris with a family of his own. And feeling some responsibility for the Carters, Stephen checked up on the family from time to time to see how they were doing. There was nothing he needed to worry about, however, as Godric had a head for business and worked hard.

"Morning," Stephen replied. "Is he still down there?" He nodded toward the tavern's door.

"I thought it best to wait until you got here, sir," Godric said. "You'll handle the unwanted attention." He grinned. "All you have to do is look at folks sideways, and that'll send them running."

"Is that what people say?" Stephen said, a bit startled.

"You've got a way of looking at people that'll freeze 'em solid, sir, if you don't mind me saying so. If it don't scare the willies out of them. Wolf's eyes, they say you've wolf's eyes."

Stephen couldn't believe any of this. But Gilbert said, "Yes, quite right. I've known mastiffs with a friendlier gaze."

"Sometimes, anyway," Godric hastened to add at Stephen's scowl; perhaps he had gone a bit too far. "Only when you're worked up about something."

"Everyone who really knows me, regards me as a most amiable fellow," Stephen said.

"Oh, yessir," Godric said. "I've said that myself many a time."

Wymar covered his mouth as if to restrain something uncomplimentary.

Stephen did not miss Wymar's disloyal gesture. But wanting to turn things away from the uncomfortable topic of what people thought of him, he said, "This is a bad business. Let's get it over with."

Godric slipped from the wagon and made his way to the door. Dyne came with him, but Godric stopped Dyne with a hand on his arm. "I'll fetch him out, sir."

Like his brother, Godric was broad-shouldered and strong armed, with thick legs, far more fit than the much older Dyne, who seemed intent on bringing out Red John's body himself as if that was a special duty. But Dyne, after some hesitation, gave way to the offer. He knew it would be hard for him to climb those tricky stairs with the dead man in his arms.

Godric opened the door and clambered down the steep steps to the dark bottom, where a white object — the linen-wrapped corpse — could be dimly seen.

"You're sure you don't need help?" Stephen called down.

"No, sir, I think I can manage!" Godric called back.

Godric knelt and gathered the body in his muscular arms. It had lost its rigidity during the night and was as limp as a wet blanket. Godric tottered one unsteady step at a time upward to the doorway, where Wymar, directed by Stephen, met him to help with the last bit of the climb. Out of breath and unsteady, Godric did not object. They lay the body gently onto the bed of the wagon.

"Well, that's that, sir," Godric said to Dyne.

"Thank you, Godric," Dyne said.

Godric climbed into the wagon. Dyne mounted his horse. Everyone looked to Stephen. He turned his horse toward Galdeford Gate, thinking how he disliked this dreadful business of dealing with the dead, determining how and why they died and who was responsible. But he had something to look forward to: tracking down dangerous criminals. Despite his disappointment and misgivings at first, the prospect was oddly exhilarating, the way he felt when he rode out on a raid.

The wagon and its party rumbled through the gate and across the wooden bridge over the town ditch into the crossroad, where at a small stone cross Galdeford Street parted into the upper and lower road, the left branch heading up eastward up the southern flank of the Titterstone Clee and the right turning southward, where after many twists and meanderings it passed through Oxford and eventually London.

Stephen went left and the others followed, a forlorn and meager party. In these troubled times, few traveled far from any town unless joined in a large group with other travelers heading the same way due to the rampant robbery small groups and single travelers faced in the wild parts of England. The road led ultimately to a river port called Bewdley and usually was well traveled. But today there were no other parties heading there, so they were on their own. Dyne could have waited for one but he had changed his mind and determined to set out straight away.

Galdeford's two streets were deserted. Even the shop windows were shuttered against the bitter wind. Then the shutters on an upper window of the Dancing Frog Tavern at the crossroad flapped open and a girl pitched the contents of a chamber pot into the street. She saw the procession and called to someone behind her at the sight of the shrouded body and another girl joined her. The first girl pointed to the wagon and its grisly cargo. They were both young and rather pretty and Wymar, not seventeen yet, could not resist the sight of such exquisite femininity, especially when it afforded a chance to show off — he mounted on a knightly steed (well, almost) and armed with sword, helmet and shield.

He waved at the girls and one of them called, "What've you got there, handsome?" as if she didn't know. Everyone in town knew about Red John's death, and it was no great puzzle who lay shrouded in the wagon when Stephen Attebrook, the town's minister of death, rode beside it.

"Wymar!" Stephen called. If Wymar had been a dog on a leash, Stephen would have snapped that leash.

"Nothing much!" Wymar called over his shoulder as they drew away from the tavern. "I'll come by later! Hey! What's your name?"

The girls giggled and leaned out of the window to watch, then pulled back because of the cold.

Presently, Upper Galdeford Road ran into Saint Mary's Way. As it made its way eastward away from town it changed its name. Some called it the Cleobury Road in honor of the fact that it ran toward Cleobury, a small market town eleven miles distant; others called it Cleehill Road, after the high hill it climbed. Eleven miles to Cleobury did not seem so far, a half day's ride for a man on horseback, but it was almost a full day for horse and wagon, and much of it was uphill, which would force a slow pace. And they had to cover six more miles after that to Fox Hall. It would be a long, uncomfortable day.

Stephen intended to use some of that time in conversation with Dyne to learn more about the circumstances of William Griffin's death. But Dyne rode behind the wagon, morose and silent, wiping away tears with the back of a hand until at last the tears ran out. From time to time, he could be heard muttering incomprehensible things, although occasionally some words could be made out, like "What will happen to us now? What indeed? It is a disaster!" It was clear he wanted to be left with his grief.

Because they were a small party and there was the possibility of bandits, Stephen had Wymar ride about fifty yards ahead to be on the lookout, while he rode with the wagon and Gilbert brought up the rear. But they met no one until the side road leading to Bitterley, a farmer leading a couple of cows. The farmer joined them until they arrived at the hamlet of Cornbrook on the slopes of the Clee, where he apparently had business. He disappeared behind one of the three hovels along a little brook while the wagon party paused for a rest and some ale that Ida and Edith Wistwode had packed for them, enjoying a spectacular view of the green landscape to the south which seemed to run on to the end of the world. They had come about halfway to Cleobury. It was three hours after sunrise. At least it wasn't as cold, although the wind on the hill carried a bite.

They plodded on. For a while the road was fairly flat but then, after a few miles, began its descent from the Clee Hill. In some places the road was quite steep, which posed its own set of challenges for the wagon. Wagons on steep descents had a habit of running out of control; the horses could not stop this, and Godric often had to strain at the brake to maintain control. Progress was slow, and there were moments where Stephen thought the brake might give way and the wagon would careen down the hill of its own accord, to crash in a ditch or hedge, pitching its cargo to the ground, if it did not overturn first, carrying the horses with it. But the brake held. It was almost a relief when the road turned uphill again after they crossed the ford at the brook below Hopton Wafers.

It was dinnertime by the time they reached Cleobury and they stopped to rest the horses at a small stone church that sat on a slight rise above the road. Gilbert thought it better to preserve what provisions they had since they couldn't know how long they would be on the road. So in an effort at economy, he led Wymar and Godric to an inn across the street. Dyne followed, delivering the surprising announcement that he would pay for everyone.

Stephen put feed bags on all the horses, but rather than entering the inn, he walked up the street to the guildhall. It was a building much like its counterpart in Ludlow, wattle and timber with a porch and first and second floors above. Stephen went inside where there was a meeting hall, also deserted. He called out and a voice replied, the words indistinct, from up a narrow, steep stairway just inside the door.

Stephen climbed the stairs to an office that sat atop the porch. A little man with wispy brown hair and a pair of Italian spectacles on his nose was working at a table that occupied almost the whole of the room. He had pen in hand, poised over a parchment roll.

"You have the look of a town clerk," Stephen said.

"I am, some of the time ... sir," the clerk said after assessing Stephen's social status from his clothing and assured manner. "How can I help you?"

"I'm looking for the hundred coroner," Stephen said.

"Oh. Do you wish to report a death?"

"No. I'm a deputy sheriff and I am looking into one."

"Ah. I see." The clerk set down the pen. "Well, Sir Hugo is up at Stottesdon for the hundred court."

"And the sheriff's bailiff?"

"There as well, I'm afraid. But perhaps I may substitute for them. I do know a bit about murder — it's rather a hobby of mine."

"Committing them, or simply an idle interest?"

"Oh, just an interest, of course. Wouldn't think of murder myself. Although I have been tempted."

"A natural temptation for one in government. Dealing with fools and all that." Stephen dug out his letter and handed to the clerk.

"Ah, you're Stephen Attebrook! I am pleased to make your acquaintance. It seems you're interested in more than one murder and robbery at the moment, I see." The clerk handed back the letter. "We have had a dreadful share of such crimes, in Shropshire, I mean. There were two on the

Bridgnorth road three and four weeks ago." The clerk shook his head. "A grisly business. The steward of Astley Abbey was accosted on the road, hacked to bits, or so I heard. And there was another in the forest above Glazeley. The lord of Quatley Manor and several retainers were similarly mutilated." The clerk frowned. "We've heard of other instances in Staffordshire as well. People slaughtered on the road. We live in dreadful times." He lowered his voice. "If only the king were back in power, these disturbances would be quelled forthwith. Do you think there is a connection between all these attacks?"

"Sheriff Alditheley seems to think so," Stephen said.

"Yes, well, it's time that someone did something about it. I suppose he means well, but he hardly has the means to collect taxes, let alone keep order. My apologies to you, though, sir. I am sure you are up to the task. Have you brought many men with you?"

"None. This is a preliminary inquiry. There was another murder outside Bewdley a couple of days ago. Have you heard anything about it?"

"Ah, yes. William Griffin of Fox Hall. Cut down on the road, so they say."

"Do you know anything about the inquiry into his death?"

"Oh, no, sir. It happened in Staffordshire, outside our jurisdiction. But as it only happened a couple of miles from Bewdley you may find out more there."

With Gilbert's and Wymar's stomachs filled with pottage that Gilbert declared was acceptable but not as good as that served at the Broken Shield, the party struggled on across the River Rea and up and down more tedious hills. They passed through several forests that made Stephen nervous, as forests were the best places for ambushes. After two hours Dyne directed Wymar to lead them up a forest road that came in from the left, and in a mile, there they were — at a small but tidy and prosperous village with a thick, forbidding forest on three sides and gentle fields on the other. A stone manor house and small church marked the northern end of the village.

"Welcome to Fox Hall," Dyne said without any welcome in his voice, just fatigue and resignation, when the wagon turned into the yard of the manor house.

Servants spilled out of the house at the sight of them, puzzled looks on their faces at the sight of only one familiar face when another had been expected and with a wagon to boot. A tall, strapping gentleman brought up the tail of the crowd. He strode through the servants with confident steps and halted at the wagon. He gazed at the shrouded body in the wagon.

"What is going on, Dyne?" the gentleman demanded. "Where's John?"

Dyne gestured to the corpse. "There, my lord."

"What?" the gentleman cried. He leaned in; his hand hovered over the shrouded corpse as if he meant to touch it, but the hand stayed poised and then withdrew. "John's *dead?* How?"

"Murdered, my lord," Dyne said. "In the most horrible way."

"I don't believe it!"

"Yet you see the proof before you, lord."

The servants began to sob loudly and cry out. "All gone! All gone!" several of them were heard to wail.

The gentleman glanced at Stephen, Gilbert and Wymar. "Who are these men?"

"The gentleman," Dyne indicated Stephen, "is Sir Stephen Attebrook of Ludlow. The other man is Gilbert Wistwode, his clerk and companion. And that young fellow is Sir Stephen's squire."

He extended a hand to Stephen. "I am Philip Galant, lord of Upper Arley Manor. It is a pleasure to meet you at last."

"You've heard of me," Stephen said. He had not expected any renown, if that's what you could call it, had penetrated into Staffordshire.

"Tongues have been wagging about you even as far away as Worcester and Kidderminster. Perhaps even in London."

"Ah," Stephen said, not sure he was happy about this.

"Yes, king's man to the core. You fought at the capture of Northampton with great distinction. I heard you even captured one of the Montfort boys. But you are most renowned as a finder extraordinaire of murderers. I am curious about the finder bit. How did you fall into that line of work?"

"I am the coroner for Munslowe Hundred. It's part of the job. Regrettably."

"He is also a deputy sheriff and has come to look into William's death," Dyne said.

Galant looked startled. "But you are from Shropshire. What gives you warrant to look into a death in Staffordshire?" By some quirk of history, a little finger of Staffordshire extended here across the River Severn, embracing the manor of Fox Hall. Had history been logical it would have fallen into Shropshire or Worcestershire.

"Sheriff Alditheley requires me look into all the killings on the roads lately in both Shropshire and Staffordshire, and, if possible, find those responsible."

"Hmm." Galant frowned. "And you are looking into John's death as well?"

"It happened in my chief jurisdiction, so, yes."

"I hope for your success. You must be fatigued. Come inside the house and rest. Will you see to John, Dyne?"

"Of course, lord."

"Well, then, shall we?"

Galant led the way into the manor house.

There was a high-backed chair, intricately carved with a crimson cushion, by the hearth fire. Galant paused behind it. He patted the back as if it was a bereaved's shoulder and then took a seat in a lesser chair next to it. He gestured to another cushioned seat on the other side of the high-backed chair that must have been reserved for distinguished visitors. "Please, sit."

Wymar, Gilbert and Godric, not bidden to sit, found seats on benches by the fire. Galant ignored them, as they were commoners.

"William was to be married next month," Galant said. He shook his head. "He found new happiness at last. His first wife died a year ago in childbirth." He sighed. "The baby did not survive either. I have never seen anyone so grief stricken. He had just emerged from it."

"I am sorry to hear that," Stephen said rather stiffly. "About the wife." He was no good at dealing with grief and had too often stood awkwardly by, feeling useless and helpless, in the face of it. And the fact the woman had died in childbirth was unnerving. He had worried terribly when his first wife, Taresa, was with child; and now there was Ida to worry about.

"What is your relationship to the Griffins?" Stephen said. "You have the air of more than just a friendly neighbor."

"I am a cousin," Galant said. "I came today expecting Dyne to return with John. He and his brother were close. We all were. We often played together as children. I thought I would do what I could to console him. Then get him drunk to forget his grief even if for only a while." Galant smiled. It was a small, wan smile of a man trying to do a difficult duty, but it lit up a face that was handsome, friendly and open, matching his charming manner; bluff and hearty.

"Your home is close?"

"Just across the Severn. Hardly a mile away."

"What do you know about William's death?"

"Only what Dyne has told me."

"And that is?"

Galant shrugged, looking both sad and outraged at the same time. "That he and his groom were attacked on the Bewdley road and cut down most savagely. I am glad you are here to do something about it. There have been altogether too many such attacks in these parts in the last year."

"Do you know where William's murder occurred?"

"I'm not sure what you mean?"

"I mean the exact place."

Galant frowned and shook his head. "I do not. All Dyne said was that the bodies were found on the road to Bewdley." He smiled thinly again.

"Has there been an inquest?"

"I don't know. I suppose there was a view of the scene, at least, because the coroner released the body for burial."

"Who would be the Staffordshire coroner responsible for the inquest?"

"That would be Richard Deme."

"Where can I find him?"

"He holds Stourton and its castle." When Stephen showed no recognition, Galant added, "It's on the other side of the river, about eight miles from my house."

"And you didn't speak to him?"

"No. I assume he came through Upper Arley, of course. It is the shortest way. We have a ferry, and he would have used it to cross the river. But he didn't stop by my house."

"In a hurry to get the unpleasant business over with," Stephen murmured.

"I suppose so." Galant frowned. "I am curious. You said you have a warrant to investigate these crimes, but you are alone."

"It is a preliminary inquiry. You mentioned a funeral for William. It hasn't taken place?"

"No, we were waiting for John's return, as I said."

"Where is the body?"

"In the chapel. Why?" Galant asked.

"Gilbert," Stephan shifted his gaze. "I think we should have our own view."

Gilbert sighed. "I was afraid you'd say that."

Galant led them across the yard to a small stone chapel that sat beside a great timber barn.

They met Dyne coming the other way. "What's going on, sir?" he asked Galant.

"I am not sure. The gentleman said something about his own view."

"Of what?" Dyne said. Then he shrugged as it came to him. "Sir Stephen is also a coroner in Shropshire. I suppose he wants to form his own opinion."

"Opinion about what?" Galant said.

"About how William met his death," Stephen said.

"But there can be no doubt! Can there?" Galant exclaimed. "You, Dyne, you saw the body! You said he had been cut to pieces! Why do you need to disturb his remains?"

"As Dyne said. To form my own opinion," Stephen said.

"You can't trust Dyne? Or our coroner?"

"Dyne will not have examined the body as I do. And your coroner is not here. In any case, he is as likely to be as wrong as anyone."

"Our coroner is an expert! A man with years of experience!"

"I am sure he is," Stephen said. "It doesn't mean he's always right."

"I will not allow this!" Galant cried.

"You do not have the authority."

"I am William's closest living relative. I have every right." Galant edged between Stephen and the chapel.

"And I wield the sheriff's authority. Get out of my way."

"Please, sir," Dyne said anxiously. "I wish you wouldn't. It's a desecration. The people won't like it. Let our beloved lord lie in peace."

"A murder investigation is not a popularity contest," Stephen said. "Often the dead give evidence against their killers." He turned his attention back to Galant. "Now, will you move or be liable for disobeying an officer of the crown?"

Galant glared. "This is outrageous! You have no warrant after our coroner already conducted a thorough examination. The sheriff shall hear about this."

"Complain all you like," Stephen said. "But stand aside."

Galant's fists clenched and unclenched. His eyes went from Stephen's feet to his black-haired head, taking in Stephen's great height, six feet, half a head taller than Galant. Galant's lips twisted, and he moved aside.

"Thank you," Stephen said. He swept by towards the chapel. Gilbert followed, eyes on the ground pretending he was not there.

Gilbert looked about the little chapel. It was large enough to hold a half dozen people: the lord and his immediate family. There were only two little slits of windows in the rounded end of the chapel and thus very little light. One body, that of Red John, lay on the ground, wrapped in linen shrouds. A coffin rested next to it, its lid on.

"I suppose we should send for a candle," Gilbert said.

"Do you want to go back out there and face Galant?" Stephen said.

"I thought I'd let you do that. You handled him so well, fetching a candle would be easy work."

Stephen had no more appetite for facing Galant than Gilbert. He crossed to the candle rack by the door, where he made a small pile of some of the straw strewn on the ground at the base of the rack. He groped in his belt pouch for his flint and steel. He flicked the flint against the steel, which sent off yellow and red sparks. It was never easy to get a fire started this way, but eventually a couple of the sparks landed on the straw pile, and it began to smolder. A little flame sprang up. Stephen lighted two candles and stomped out the fire so that there was no danger of it spreading to the rest of the straw upon the chapel floor.

Stephen set the candles on the altar and turned to the coffin. He tried the lid but it had been nailed shut. He went to the chapel door. Dyne and Galant had apparently returned to the manor house, but there was a luckless servant passing from the barn to the house.

"Fetch me a hammer and a pry bar!" he shouted at the servant, who turned in surprise.

"Me?" the servant stammered.

"You! And don't waste any time at it."

The servant scampered toward the smithy.

Stephen waited in the doorway to keep an eye on him in case he decided that some other task demanded his immediate attention. But the servant returned in short order with the hammer and bar.

"What do you need with these, sir?" the servant asked suspiciously.

"My companion needs a tooth extracted," Stephen said and shut the door in the man's face.

"You didn't need to be so sharp with the poor fellow," Gilbert said.

"I'm in a bad mood."

Stephen thought about having Gilbert do the next bit, but knowing that it would provoke a sour comment and protest that he did not feel like having to respond to, he dropped the hammer and went to work with the pry bar, moving slowly so as not to damage the coffin any more than necessary. He gradually worked his way around so the nails came out and he lifted the lid.

The body of a heavy-set man with reddish hair — not the same brilliant red as John's — lay in the coffin unshrouded apart from the fact a linen napkin had been laid upon his face. Stephen removed the napkin and saw there were numerous deep slashes upon the head and a face that may have once been comely but was now so damaged that it was a mishmash of chopped meat, the teeth showing through the mangled cheeks. One arm had been hacked off, and lay upon the body. He had not, as Dyne said, been hacked to pieces, not counting the severed arm, but he had been treated cruelly. There were other wounds, cuts and thrusts in his chest and stomach, visible as rents in his clothing. Some looked like sword wounds but a few looked as though they had been administered with an axe. Ordinarily a body was stripped of its clothing, washed and redressed for burial when the deceased was the lord of a manor, but it looked as though no one wanted to confront these frightful injuries. They'd simply put William Griffin in his box in the clothes in which he died. Fortunately, the smell was not too bad, since the weather had been cool.

"I wonder where the groom is," Stephen said. He hadn't thought of this until now. "The one who died with him. We should have a look at him, too."

"I think poor William is enough for one day," Gilbert said grimly through clenched teeth. He was used to the dead, but seeing a corpse in this condition was stomach churning. "Probably buried already, anyway. I do not fancy having to dig him up to satisfy your curiosity."

Stephen did not fancy having to dig up the dead any more than Gilbert. "Let's get him out and this over with," he said.

"We're not going to do the usual, are we?" Gilbert asked.

"I think we can tell what killed him," Stephen said. "We'll do what we did with Red John. Just to check if there is anything else that may tell us anything."

Gilbert stepped reluctantly to the foot of the coffin where he grasped the corpse's ankles, that being easier to lift than the shoulders.

Together they lifted the body and set it on the rushes.

Stephen raised the severed arm from the body and examined the wound. It was a clean cut just above the elbow through the bone of the upper arm. He set the forearm aside and took a moment to examine the wound to the arm itself.

Stephen murmured, "Made with a good sharp sword."

He now turned his attention to the nature of the other wounds. "Look here," he said. "All the cuts are at right angles to the spine. If Griffin had been standing, most if not all of them would be at sharper angles." Stephen made a diagonal chopping motion to demonstrate what he meant.

"So he was lying down when he was mutilated," Gilbert said. "Perhaps after he was already dead."

"I'd say so. And see here — I count only six slashes on the right side but so many on the left that it's impossible to count them."

Gilbert digested this information without comment. He said, "What do you think killed him, then, if not these blows to the head and body?"

"Let's turn him over."

Stephen rolled the body onto its stomach. There was a puncture in the cloth of the dead man's coat about the level of the shoulder blades.

"Damn it, I should have done this first," Stephen said. He rolled the body onto its back so he could unbuckle the man's belt, then rolled him over again. Stephen pulled up the coat and linen shirt beneath it so they could see the bare skin. Two wounds stood out, black encrusted, against a purpling skin. They were about an inch wide with a ragged edge, not clean punctures like that made by a sword or a dagger.

"Arrows," Stephen decided. "He was shot in the back. Looks like a hunting arrow, too."

"Ah," Gilbert murmured. "How can you be so certain?"

"Whoever shot him pulled them out. Hunting arrows have broad heads to catch in the wound. This makes them hard to pull out, which explains the ragged nature of the punctures."

"I daresay, the work of a spendthrift killer," Gilbert said. "Arrows are expensive."

"I'd have done the same. If just to recover the heads so they could be reused."

"Shot in the back while on his horse and savagely used on the ground. That face, it is the stuff of nightmares. Why would someone do such a thing? It speaks of such hate and malice."

"And everyone liked the Griffins. Or so they say." Stephen moved to the corpse's head. "We've seen enough. Let's get him back in his box and let William rest in peace at last."

Supper that evening was subdued and awkward. Dyne sat wrapped in his own gloomy thoughts, now and then casting a reproachful glance at Stephen and Gilbert. He resisted being drawn out about what he had seen at the death place and the discovery of the bodies.

Galant stayed for supper but was no more interested in conversation than Dyne. He hadn't gotten over his anger at Stephen's failure to heed his desires about viewing William Griffin's corpse and he spat out brief replies from behind an icy reserve. Galant shrugged when Stephen asked about the groom, and said shortly, "I only know what Dyne told me. I never saw him myself."

Stephen found out more, however, after supper. Ralph, the village hayward, came up while the household servants were preparing to retire for the night.

"Sir, can I have a word," Ralph said quietly as the servants spread out their pallets by the hall's hearth fire, and Galant and Dyne climbed the stairs to chambers above the hall.

"Certainly," Stephen said.

They went outside into the yard, which was dim with the overcast and the fading sun.

"You asked about Tad," Ralph said.

"He is?" Stephen said.

"The boy who died with Lord William, sir."

"Ah, of course. What about him? Did you see the body?"

Ralph nodded. "I went with Master Dyne."

"You were among those who found them, then?"

"There were only the two of us. And I remained with them through the night until the coroner came on Sunday."

"Dyne said they were all cut to pieces."

Ralph gulped. "They were, well, sort of."

"What do you mean, sort of?"

"The boy wasn't savaged like Lord William. He'd been stabbed once in the heart, was all, according to what I saw." He let out a long breath. "There've been rumors of many such killings hereabout. Highborn people, clerics, merchants, mutilated. But here's the thing, sir. They say that while many common people have been robbed and even killed, they were not used like Lord William."

"So it's only the rich who are violated," Stephen said.

"That's what I've heard, sir. You're likely to find out more tomorrow when the neighbors come for the funerals." Ralph glanced toward the house. "Well, sir. Time I got home."

Chapter 6

Ida awoke early on the morning Stephen and Gilbert were to leave for Fox Hall.

She fought back a bout of nausea while Stephen snored beside her. It was growing light so dawn was not that far off: a cock cleared its throat in the yard next door.

She slipped out of bed, pulled on a linen shift then a cloak, and tiptoed downstairs to make a last-minute check of all the provisions she had collected to ensure that they were properly packed away for loading onto the pack horses, as if overnight fairies might have crept in and ruined all her work. Nothing had been disturbed. It was all as she left it the evening before.

She thought about returning to bed to savor Stephen's warmth and the closeness of him, for he was likely to be gone a long time. It was the lot of a gentry wife to be alone when her husband was off on some business. The other times Stephen had gone away, she had endured the separation stoically, but this one felt different. She was filled with dread and foreboding because of the job he had to do, searching for a band of vicious robbers and murderers without any help. Gilbert and Wymar were good men, but in a fight they could not be relied upon. Stephen considered himself to be careful and cunning but she knew better. In fact, he was often maddeningly reckless. The memory of him bursting through the ceiling of the house in which she was held captive to free her from a kidnapping (an experience that haunted her yet) was still fresh, as was his near death at the battle of Northampton last year — not to mention the terrible risks he had taken leading the party in the recapture of Ludlow Castle last December. The intervening months had been quiet, with nothing more to worry about than whether the food stocks of their manor would see everyone through to spring; not even a murder disturbed the relative calm. She hoped this state of affairs would continue. But it was not to be.

When Ida reached the foot of the stairs, Joan sat up and smoothed back her long hair.

"Is that you, Ida?" Joan said. "What are you doing up? Sarah, the fire!" It was Sarah's job, as the housekeeper, to get the fire going.

"It's not even dawn yet," Sarah's voice came from the outer darkness. "All right, all right. I'm coming."

"I'll take care of it," Ida said. "You two stay where you are."

Ida removed the pottery cover from the coals, glad to find it still warm. She laid a hand over the ashes. They were warm too. Using the little iron ash shovel she uncovered the surviving coals beneath the ashes and dropped a handful of hay on them. The hay smoked for a moment, then burst into flame. Ida stacked a square tower of kindling about the tinder and sat on the nearby bench to watch the fire grow before adding a few logs. It was good to be warm. Summer couldn't get here fast enough.

As it grew warmer in the hall, Wymar rose and staggered past on his way to the privy. "Morning, m'lady," he muttered, still half asleep.

Sarah and Joan were not out of their beds when the four boys — Harry's son John, Sarah's sons Theo and Johnnie, and Christopher, who was now a precocious four — were up and kneeling by the fire, thirsty for its warmth.

"I'm hungry," Christopher said.

"You're always hungry, you little runt," Johnnie said.

"You'd eat a raw rat, given the chance" John agreed.

"No, I won't. I'd have Sarah cook it first," Christopher said.

"Rat pie," Theo grinned. "Delicious."

John laughed and swatted Christopher on the back of his black-haired head. Christopher responded by trying to push the much bigger boy over. Both Johns then ganged up on Christopher. Joan was out of bed in a flash and pulled the boys apart by the scruffs of their necks.

"No roughhousing near the fire!" Joan said. "How often do you have to be told?"

"I'll fetch some breakfast," Sarah said, rising and wrapping herself in her blanket.

"What's all the shouting about?" Stephen inquired sleepily from the top of the stairs.

"Nothing to bother yourself about," Ida said. "Come down. Sarah's getting breakfast."

Ida watched Stephen, Gilbert and Wymar plod down Bell Lane. As they passed into Broad Street, she went back inside the house. She climbed to her bedchamber and changed into a rough brown woolen gown, riding gloves, thick socks and sturdy shoes. Cloaked again, she returned to the hall.

Joan, by the fire sipping warm cider, asked with narrowed eyes, "Are you going somewhere?"

"We are going to the manor," Ida said. "Make ready. I want to get an early start."

"Why are we doing that?" Joan asked.

"It's Wednesday," Ida said. "Stephen always visits the manor on Wednesday. Since he is otherwise occupied, the duty falls to me." Whenever possible, Stephen went to Halton Priors Manor to check on the work going on and to review the manor's accounts. It wasn't that he didn't trust their co-stewards, Randulfus and Frances Bartelott, but he still felt it was essential to keep a close watch on things so the necessary work got done as required and their money wasn't being misspent. Many a lord who failed to take such precautions and was ill served by his steward found himself in debt and ruin.

"That's not wise," Joan said.

"No, it isn't," said Sarah.

"I don't see why it isn't," Ida said. "It's only three miles. What can possibly happen in so little a distance."

"A lot," Joan said. "You know how unsettled the countryside is. You could be *taken* again. It won't be for," she lowered her voice so the children couldn't hear, "*rape* this time, but it will be for ransom. You would fetch a fortune in ransom. Everyone in the county knows how much Stephen fancies you."

"I should not like to be the man who kidnaps me for ransom," Ida said coldly, trying to conceal how cold the prospect of being held for ransom made her feel. Such a fate could ruin the family financially.

"She's right," Sarah said. "There's plenty of barons' supporters around here who would like a crack at you."

Ida sank onto her chair, her mouth an obstinate line. Her impulse was to reject this advice and march across Bell Lane to the stable at the Broken Shield Inn, where the family kept its horses. But she knew her friends were right, much as she didn't want to admit it. Two women riding alone in the country would be easy pickings for any scoundrel. She could be snatched by someone living rough in the forest upon Bridgewood Chase, the long hill south of the manor that ran along the road for miles (although she had not heard there was anyone doing so), and then sold to another well placed to demand a ransom. There were at least two gentry families near Leintwardine who were for the barons, and the last time they had come to a Ludlow market, members of both had snubbed her and Stephen. They were just the sort to play such a game.

While she struggled with the sensibility of what she had been told, Sarah finished giving breakfast to the family and the boys went off to help Harry harness his pony to his cart, since he had more deliveries to make that morning. Sarah filled a pot with water and set about cutting up a shank of mutton for the pot. A variety of vegetables went under her knife after that and then into the pot along with some barley to simmer through the morning. There was nothing fancy about this dish — it was only a simple pottage, but it was all they could afford. Joan sat across the fire and watched Ida as if in preparation to wrestle her to the floor if she made a bid for the door. Christopher returned alone from the yard, kicking disconsolately at the dirt. Harry had sent him back as too young to help with the deliveries. Sarah directed him into a corner where his toys were kept in a wooden box and soon he was playing with a wooden horse and rider, muttering things like, "I am a valiant knight! Take that!", stuff he couldn't get away within the hearing of the older boys.

Ida began to pace beside the hearth fire. If she couldn't get to the manor, there had to be something important she could do, something beyond housekeeping, important as that was (without it no one would be fed, clothed or have a decent place to sleep). And then it came to her: she could conduct the inquiry Stephen planned to make into the death of Red John Griffin.

"Get your cloak," Ida said to Joan.

"You're not still thinking about making for the manor, are you?" Joan said.

"No. We have other work to do."

Ida marched uphill toward the mouth of Raven Lane, Joan at her side.

"What do you have in mind?" Joan said. It was obviously not a shopping expedition. They had brought no baskets for that.

"The night watch!" Ida said.

"What?" Joan said, bewildered.

"We are going to question the night watch!"

"What for — oh! This is about Red John." You would never lose a bet on Joan's intelligence.

"Precisely," Ida said, turning into Raven Lane. "Stephen told me he needed to talk to them. Since he is not here to do that, I will do it for him. Perhaps we may solve the riddle of the murder ourselves."

"I *seeeeee* …." Joan said, not altogether certain about what might be accomplished.

"Oh, come on. It will be fun."

"I've heard Stephen complaining about the tedium of investigations more than I have the fun of them."

"Well, it will be fun for us no matter how tedious."

"Tedious fun. That's something new."

There was a Crooked Man

The first problem was to determine who the watchmen were and where they could be found. Ida knew only the vaguest things about them. There were eight, selected once a year for the post. Two men at a time patrolled the town for two hours, when they retired and two others took up the patrols, so there were four patrols throughout the night. Nights were longer in the autumn through spring, so the predawn hours were left unwatched because it was thought that evildoers were so worn out by drink and debauchery they would be unconscious; and it was cold. Besides, the town had to pay the watchmen and even eight of them was considered a great expense. Yet the money allotted was not enough for a man to live on, so all the watchmen pursued a craft during the day. She just had to discover who they were and where they could be found. Harry probably knew, but she had let him get away before she had a chance to ask him about it.

Raven Lane emptied into High Street, a broad open space that stretched from the castle gate to Broad Street. It was the town's marketplace during market days, when it was festive and busy, but today it was deserted and rather forlorn looking. There were a few shops with their shutters down in the hopes of attracting business, but most were closed against the cold wind that swept down from the north.

Ida clutched her hood about her face and struck out across High Street for the guildhall on the other side.

The hall, where the town bailiff and aldermen conducted business, was a three-story timber and wattle building coated with startlingly white plaster, freshly applied last summer, so it gleamed even in the dark. The upper floors jutted over a large porch supported by timber columns. In better weather the town's sub-bailiffs could often be found lounging there on benches. But today the benches were vacant.

As was to be expected, the four bailiffs were in the hall seated on stools and benches before the great fireplace, enjoying a fire. That fireplace, one of the few in town, had been added to one wall of the hall at great expense just over a year ago, which required an extra levy of the town's burgages.

Protestations that the town's bridges needed more attention than a new fireplace for the hall went unheeded; the comfort of the aldermen during their deliberations was deemed more important than the safety of travelers crossing the seven bridges leading into town.

One of them heard the women enter the hall and he stood up quickly as he recognized who it was. "Boys, we've a visitor."

The others rose rapidly in surprise and there was a chorus of "my lady."

"What can we do for you, m'lady," asked Thomas, an elderly man with a pot belly and furry ears, who as the oldest and longest serving bailiff was generally seen as the senior man (although two of the others disputed this, arguing that he had grown forgetful and negligent in his old age).

"I would like the names of the men on the night watch and where each of them can be found," Ida said.

"I, er, why would you want to know that?" Thomas said, hastening to add, "if you don't mind my asking?"

"I would like to speak to them," Ida said.

"About what?" asked a perplexed Thomas.

Ida had not expected to be asked about her reasons — common people were not in the habit of asking gentry why they wanted something. But rather than barking an order or issuing a rebuke, she drew herself up to make herself seem taller than she was (a difficult feat since she was only two inches over five feet in height).

"My husband's duties as a deputy sheriff have taken him away from town. He has asked me to make inquiries into the death of John Griffin while he is indisposed," she said. "Stephen wants the night watch questioned, among others. While memories are fresh."

"I don't know as they know anything," Thomas said haltingly. "Otherwise I'm sure they'd have said something."

"I must ask them myself, nonetheless," Ida said.

Thomas shuffled his feet. His fingers knotted and unknotted. "Well, m'lady, traipsing about town to speak to strange men isn't the sort of thing a lady ought to do. Apart from the *impropriety* of it, it smacks — it smacks of *manual labor*. Almost, like."

"I'll be the guardian of my own virtue," Ida said.

"Yes, yes, I'm sure, m'lady," Thomas said, although he was not convinced.

The bailiffs regarded the two women. They were the same height, about the same age, the same slender build and had the same coloring, blonde hair, neatly concealed by pill hats and veils, blue eyes and milky white skin. Indeed, they looked so much alike that some people thought they were sisters. But there was a whiff of iron about the both of them. And the fact both carried rather large daggers had not gone unnoticed or unremarked in town. It was not unknown for a woman to be armed, but usually she kept the weapon out of sight. These two carried the daggers on their belts in quick, easy reach. Everyone in town knew why they did so — both had been kidnapped by a gang intent on selling them to the infidels in North Africa and they hadn't gotten over the fear of it happening again. Some whispered that they had been cruelly violated, but that was only speculation.

"Well," Thomas said, "them daggers might protect you from unwanted advances, but they'll do nothing about what the gossips will say."

"I cannot control what the gossips say, but I am free to ignore it."

"I reckon you should," Thomas said. "No good comes from heeding a wagging tongue. Let's see, there's Raymond Stantone, he's a weaver. His shop is on Mill Street by the gate. Then there's Warin Lingen. He's a painter. His house is in Tower Street. Then …." The list ran on to include John Warewyk, a dyer on Silk Mill Lane; Henry Ewyas, a weaver on Corve Street by the gate; Richard Cachepol, the chief assistant at the mill below Mill Gate; Henry Pirefeld, a bottle maker, with a shop on Old Street by the gate; William Munselowe, a cheesemonger in the Bull Ring; and Hugh Dounton, a fuller, also on Mill Street.

"Thank you kindly, Master Thomas," Ida said when he finished.

"My pleasure, m'lady," Thomas said. "Good luck to you."

Four of the watch lived near the Bull Ring, which was closer than the bottom of Mill Street, where the others lived, so they went there first. Ludlow was a small town and it was only a three or four minute walk. Neither Lingen, the painter; Pirefeld, the bottlemaker; Ewyas, the weaver; nor Munselowe, the cheesemonger reported anything untoward happening on their watches.

"There was the usual drunks to deal with," Munselowe, who had the first watch with Ewyas, said over the counter of his shop after being disappointed that Ida had not come to buy any cheese. "You know, the folks who've had a bit too much and don't want to leave. We have to go round to all the taverns to make sure they've shut their doors and sent everyone home. And it's usually the same lot. The drunks, I mean. None put up a fight, though."

"You don't arrest them for being out after curfew?" Ida asked.

"Na, lady. I'd have no friends in town if I did that. We just shoo them along."

"Didn't you have to help one of them home that night?" said Munselowe's wife, Magota.

"Oh, yeah. Bill Chode. Had another argument with his wife and took it out on an ale pitcher. Couldn't walk a step for falling down. But that was it. It was a quiet night, our part of it. No noisier than usual, anyway."

"Did you go by the Blue Duck?" Ida asked.

"'Course," Munselowe said.

"Nothing out of the ordinary there? Did you speak to Red John?"

"We had a word. Two lads were leaving as we got there and I asked if he had any left. He said he didn't, and that was that."

"When you say, 'that was that,' what do you mean?"

"That he closed the door and barred it, same as usual."

"Is that the only way down to the tavern, through that door?"

"No, there's a trap door that opens into the floor above. Red John didn't use it much, though, far as I know, once he lost his chamber there. Mistress Estrill, she lives above, a poor widow, wouldn't let him up."

"Thank you, Master Munselowe. You've been most helpful."

"Begging your pardon, m'lady, but isn't it a bit … unseemly for you to be asking about such matters?"

"You know, women of my station have been called upon to defend castles in wartime when their husbands are away," Ida said. "This is no different."

"If you say so, m'lady."

Ida left the shop with Joan, feeling the tongues already beginning to wag on this side of town.

The shutters on Stantone's shop were closed because of the cold. Ida pushed the door open, causing a small bell on the inside door handle to ring, hardly audible even in the passage over the clatter of looms within the shop. A heavy-set woman who apparently had a dog's sharp ears appeared at the shop's inner door to see who had arrived.

"Ah, my lady," she said. "What brings you here?" Weavers usually did not do business with the ordinary people of the town. They wove fabrics on commission for others, like drapers, who sold their work.

"I've come to speak with Richard Stantone. Is he too busy to see me?" Ida asked.

The woman frowned, a formidable grimace that said Ida should go away and not bother with them. "He most decidedly is busy. What do you want with him, anyway?"

"I have a few questions about what he might have seen while on watch the night Red John Griffin was killed."

"I see. And why does this concern you?"

Ida gave her short speech about making an inquiry on Stephen's behalf. The heavy woman did not seem any more convinced of the rightness of it than the bailiffs had been. But she backed away and gestured to a young man across the room who was busy at a vertical loom; two other women labored away at horizontal looms whose square frames were so large that there was little spare room in the shop. The young man, alerted to the disturbance, turned to see what it was about. He was much younger than Ida had expected, perhaps only as old as she was (she would turn eighteen soon), a slender lad with auburn hair, a freckled face and no beard. She thought Stantone would be a grown man and owner of the shop. But that was a mistake. He had to be an apprentice and the heavy woman was either the owner of the shop or the owner's wife.

Ida made her way around the horizontal looms with the heavy woman in close pursuit.

Stantone stopped working as Ida came up. But the heavy woman barked, "Keep at it! You can work while you talk!"

"He hasn't the wit for that," one of the other weavers said.

"He'll have to do his best," the heavy woman said. "He lost an hour this morning, sleeping late, the sluggard. I'll not have him lose more time now."

If Stephen had been here instead, Ida suspected that he would say something sharp in his command voice that would knock the heavy woman on her heels. But Ida had no such command voice, nor did she think that she would get far by shooting orders about. She was small and felt she couldn't intimidate a housecat.

"Will it bother your work if I ask you a few questions while you're busy?" she asked Stantone. "I'll try not to interfere."

"No, m'lady," Stantone said in a squeaky voice. "I can manage, no matter what the others think. What do you want to know?"

"I'm interested in the night Red John Griffin was killed," Ida said. "Can you first tell me which watch you stood?"

"I'm on the fourth watch this month," Stantone said.

"I take it you're an apprentice here. What's an apprentice doing on the night watch?" Such a thing was very unusual. Apprentices were under the thumbs of their masters who were reluctant to allow it since it could mean a loss of their labor if they were tired during the day, which frequently was the case.

Stantone glanced at the heavy woman. "Mistress Rydelere volunteered me."

"Ah." Ida saw at least one thing more clearly. Rydelere was the shop owner. She had put Stantone forward for the watch in order to pocket his stipend.

"Your rounds, do they take you by the Blue Duck?"

"Certainly. We walk the entire town, unlike what some people think."

"What time did you pass the Blue Duck?"

"I don't know, probably during the first hour and then the last. It does take a while to walk the town, you know, but we usually get down each street at least twice."

"And nothing untoward happened during your watch? You saw no one about?"

"Well, there was the vagrant."

"Vagrant?" Ida asked.

"Yeah, we catch them from time to time. You know, poor people without a home, hiding out in town, hoping to do some unlicensed begging in the morning."

"Tell me about this vagrant," Ida said.

"Well, she was the most pathetic thing. No more than eleven or twelve and skinny as a nail. We found her in Old Street." Stantone frowned. "It was across from the Blue Duck. On Master Hobjohn's doorstep."

"When was this?"

"Toward the end of the second hour."

"Where is she now?"

"I have no idea."

"You didn't arrest her?"

"No. People like that can't pay a fine, and if you gaol them, they're just an unwanted expense."

"What did you do with her, then?"

"Dounton and I put her out through Galdeford Gate, since it was right around the corner."

"Did you get her name?"

"She said it was Iveta."

Iveta was her name …. Ida wondered if the girl had seen anything. Had she been right across the street earlier, when the murder happened? Ida didn't know enough about the habits of vagrants to have an opinion.

"What do you think, Joan?" Ida asked after they had left the shop. "Do you think it's worth the effort to try and find that girl?"

"What would Stephen do?" Joan asked.

"He would look for her, I suppose." Ida had little exposure to the tedium of Stephen's work and she experienced a stab of sympathy at how awful his work could be. The poor man. "If you were this Iveta, what would you do?"

Joan rubbed a shapely chin with a long-fingered hand. "If the watch found her wandering the streets, I'd say she just arrived in town. If it was me, I'd try to find someone who'd take me in. If she's able-bodied, she could work. A little girl like that could survive on scraps. Perhaps she's found a place already."

"So we first have to find out where she went after she was thrown out of town." The enormity of the problem of finding Iveta began to sink in. Ida realized she'd have to enquire of every household in town. That was impossible. Even if she made that inquiry, most likely Iveta saw nothing at all and the effort would be wasted.

"You know," Joan said, "I heard there's another family of vagrants living under the Galdeford Gate bridge. They might know something."

There was a Crooked Man

"I suppose we must inquire," Ida said. It wasn't far up the hill to High Street from here, but she was exhausted and it seemed like a great mountain to her aching feet.

Chapter 7

Ida was winded from the swift walk up to Galdeford Gate, and she and Joan paused at the gate's tunnel-like passageway to catch their breath and ease aching feet. They had been standing and walking all morning and wanted to sit down more than anything.

The pause was unfortunate, however, as it prompted One-eye Dick to shuffle over, his bowl held out before him in shaking hands.

"Surely, you can spare a farthing!" Dick said in his raspy voice.

"Leave the ladies alone!" Old Rick, one of the gate wardens, snapped from the comfort of his niche. "Get back or I'll see you thrashed."

"My, we are testy today," Dick said. "Shit got stuck in yer bum again?"

"If you don't get back to your proper place, I'll have yer license," Old Rick said. "Begging away from yer spot — that's a major infraction!"

Dick grumbled something unintelligible, just as well as it probably was wildly profane, and shuffled back to his place ten yards inside the gate.

"Going for a walk, Lady Attebrook?" Old Rick said. "Not the day for it. Nasty. Cold."

Ida glanced toward the wooden bridge on the other side of the passageway. "Do you remember Richard Stantone and Hugh Dounton putting out a young girl the night of Red John's murder?"

Old Rick stroked a chin that needed shaving. "That would be Monday night."

"Yes."

"I did hear one of the boys talking about it."

"Boys?"

"The others on the tower guard, my lady."

"Do you know what happened to her?"

"Her?"

"The girl. The one put out of town."

"Oh, I'm sure she went on her way. Back to wherever she belongs. Wherever that is."

"Thank you," Ida said. "You've been such a help."

Old Rick beamed, showing off two rows of badly crooked teeth.

Ida strode out onto the bridge. As she reached the center of the span, she detected low voices coming from beneath the bridge, which stopped abruptly.

She went a few feet northward to get a better view of what might lie under the bridge. The ditch itself was V-shaped and about ten feet deep. The steep slopes were covered with a carpet of knee-high grass. Here and there a few weeds and saplings had popped up. The town was required to keep the ditch clear, but due to the expense, that obligation was often neglected. Beneath the bridge an indentation had been dug into the Galdeford side and the soil thrown into the ditch bottom to create a level place. There was a tent of sorts in the indentation, a canvas awning supported by slender wooden poles. Ida could see two sets of feet projecting from beneath the awning.

Ida thought about calling out to the owners of those feet, but she was unsure how they would react — would they ignore her? She had not thought much about this ditch in the past, but now the prospect of having to clamber down its precipitous sides loomed before her, she was having second thoughts about it. It was steep and easy to slip to the bottom.

Taking a deep breath and summoning the courage to disregard the embarrassment if anyone saw what she was about, Ida stepped into the ditch.

"Wait," Joan said. "You're not thinking of going down there, are you? It's not right. Let me go."

"No, it is my task, however, unpleasant," Ida said.

She slipped over the edge and grasped tufts of grass and random saplings for support as she made her way down. But her precautions failed. Her feet slipped and she tumbled to the bottom, losing her hat and veil and getting soaked at the bottom; water from recent rains had not fully drained away.

She struggled to her feet, her back and legs wet.

"That was gracefully done," Joan said.

"I'll bet you can't do better," Ida said.

"I'll take that bet."

Joan came down much more steadily than Ida and reached bottom without mishap. She retrieved Ida's hat and, removing strands of grass from Ida's hair, replaced the hat. Her mouth turned down in disapproval.

"It will have to do," Joan said. "But what will people say now?"

Meanwhile, the owners of the feet, alerted by the tumult, peered around the canvas of their tent at their visitors. They were a pair of young men with ragged beards and dirt-smeared faces. They were clad in coats and stockings that were so patched that it was hard to believe they had started out as a single garment.

"What you doing here?" one of the boys said. "Who're you?"

Ida waded through the marshy grass to the level place beneath the bridge.

"I am Ida Attebrook," Ida said.

The mention of her name had no effect on them; unlike most everyone in Ludlow, they had no idea who she was.

The eyes of one of the boys narrowed. "I bet she's got a purse in there," he said, targeting her belt pouch. "Come on. No one will see."

"You're daft," the other said. "It's broad daylight. All the bitch has to do is call out and the guard will be on us."

"I don't know," the first one said. "I'm damned hungry."

He took a step forward. Ida put a hand on her dagger.

"You couldn't hurt a fly with that little pig sticker," he said, grinning maliciously.

"Maybe she can't," Joan said from behind Ida. "But you'll have trouble dealing with two of us."

The first one chewed his lower lip. "Oh, come on. I was just having a bit of fun. What are you ladies doing down here anyway? We don't see many of your ilk in our little castle."

"I'm looking for someone. A girl named Iveta," Ida said.

She thought she saw a flash of recognition in their eyes, but the second one said, "Who's Iveta?"

"She's a vagrant. She was thrown out of town night before last," Ida said. "About two hours before dawn. Did you hear anything? Did you see her?"

"We sleep like logs," the first boy said. "Don't know anything about no Iveta."

"I'll bet you don't," Ida said. She dug in her purse for halfpenny, which she tossed at their feet. It hurt to do this; every penny was precious in the Attebrooks' current predicament.

The boys scrambled for the halfpenny. The second one got it first, and the other boy promptly disarmed him of it.

"Next time you see her, tell her that Ida Attebrook wants to speak to her," Ida said. "I live in Bell Lane, the house across from the Broken Shield Inn."

The first boy bit the penny, assuring himself that it was indeed silver.

"Careful you don't swallow it," Joan said.

"Will there be more like this if she turns up?" the first boy asked.

"Maybe," Ida said.

Chapter 8

Early in the morning neighbors began trickling in for the funeral. None of them had heard about Red John's death and they were aghast to learn it would be a double burial.

The ceremonies were set for midday, with a dinner afterwards that the manor's cooking staff labored through the night and into the morning to prepare. The manor's grooms hurried about greeting the visitors and taking care of their horses, which needed to be fed and watered, which took place in a temporary paddock behind the barn.

Godric, meanwhile, had decided to return straightaway to Ludlow even though there was no traveling party for him to join. Stephen felt guilty about leaving him to make the journey alone, so he had ordered Wymar to go with him.

Godric's horses were also let loose there and they chose that morning to be fractious and uncooperative, running away when he approached them with halters and ropes. The grooms paid no attention to this trouble, since Godric was a mere hired man and was presumed to be able to care for his own business. Wymar, who was to escort Godric back to town, had no trouble collecting and tacking his own horse, and he watched Godric's struggles with amusement, shouting unhelpful suggestions on what to do until Stephen sent him to the kitchen for a pair of dried apples. When Wymar returned, Stephen tossed the apples to Godric, who used them to entice his ponies so that he could get them haltered and then hitched to his wagon.

As Godric and Wymar headed down the lane toward the Bewdley road, Stephen spotted the hayward driving in a cart with more hay for the guests' horses.

"Have you time to spare after this chore?" Stephen asked Ralph as he and one of his boys dumped hay over the paddock fence.

"What do you have in mind, sir?" Ralph asked, leaning on his pitchfork.

"I want you to show me where you found Lord William."

"I'll have to ask Dyne if he can spare me for the rest of the morning, sir. We are rather busy, so I wouldn't get your hopes up."

But Ralph returned shortly from the house and nodded that Dyne had given his assent. Stephen saddled his horse and Gilbert's, while Ralph looked after one for himself, and in less than a quarter of an hour, they also took to the lane leading southward away from the manor.

At the Bewdley road, Ralph led them left toward the town, which, he said, lay another three miles away through a thick forest that engulfed the road so that it seemed little more than a tunnel through overhanging oak and chestnut branches. It was quiet, serene, disturbed only by the twitter of birds, the rustling of red squirrels among the leaf litter, and the clop of the horses' hooves.

Ralph reined up about a mile into the forest. He pointed to a spot at the base of a large beech tree. "We found him here," he said.

"And the groom?" Stephen said, dismounting.

"Tad was back that way about thirty yards," Ralph said. "What are you expecting to find, sir, if you don't mind my asking?"

"I don't know. You never know until you look."

Stephen snooped about, hoping, but not expecting the disturbed ground to tell him something about the attackers. He found nothing out of the ordinary: wagon and cart tracks, hoof marks, a few footprints, mostly old, nothing that could be linked to the attackers.

He straightened up from his study, thinking hard. "Was Griffin going to Bewdley or coming from it, do you think."

"I'm sure coming from it," Ralph said. "He left for Bewdley well before dinner — his plan was to eat with Ingrede Paddoc. Yet the horses came back a couple of hours after dinner."

"Midafternoon, then," Stephen said.

"Yes," Ralph agreed.

Stephen looked up and down the road from the spot where William's body was found.

"He was shot in the back, you know, Lord William. Hit with two arrows."

Ralph's mouth fell open. "I did not know this."

"And Tad, the groom. He was also shot with an arrow?"

"I don't know," Ralph said.

"Did you see the coroner examine him? Here?"

Ralph nodded.

"Did the coroner remove Tad's clothing to look for wounds?"

"No, he didn't," Ralph said.

"Not even lifting his coat and shirt?"

"Not that I saw."

"Not very thorough," Gilbert murmured.

"So, we don't know," Stephen said to himself. "But I'd say it's likely."

Stephen looked again down the road toward Bewdley. Shot in the back ... the words ran through is mind. The only way this could have happened is if the attackers let Griffin and the groom pass and then come out onto the road behind them.

"Thirty yards, wouldn't you say, Gilbert?" Stephen said as Gilbert came up.

"Thirty yards for what?"

"It's the distance most men can shoot a bow and hope to hit a target with any degree of accuracy."

"If you say so," Gilbert said. "You know more about such things than I."

"Come on," Stephen said.

He paced off thirty yards and stopped. "You take that side." He indicated the north side of the road. "I'll take that one."

"What are we looking for?"

"Where our attackers lay in wait. They'll have left some sign it. Trampled, disturbed leaves if nothing else."

Gilbert pushed into the wood, muttering something about wild goose chases and having better things to do, like breakfast, which he had been forced to forgo except for a scrap of bread and handful of nuts. Stephen pressed into the forest on the other side of the road. He roamed about, first toward the place where the body was found, and finding nothing of interest, he headed away from it. Everything here, unfortunately, looked perfectly forest-like. If the leaves had been disturbed by ambushers, he couldn't tell..

"Stephen!" Gilbert called. "I've found something."

Stephen hurried across the road. Gilbert came around a great old oak, its trunk so wide that a man holding his hands out could not be seen behind it.

"What is it?" Stephen asked.

Gilbert held out a brown leather bottle. "I found this behind the tree. There."

The bottle was new, the leather stiff and without the scratches and abrasions of use. Stephen sniffed the open mouth, for there was no stopper, and smelled sour ale. There was a maker's mark on the bottom, an acorn surrounded by small oak leaves.

"Just behind this oak?" he asked, almost not believing Gilbert.

"Right there. As I said." Gilbert pointed again. "Among the roots."

"Curious that someone would lose so valuable an object." Leather bottles were common objects; many travelers had something similar. But even something so common had a cost and was not willingly abandoned.

Stephen stepped around the tangle of roots at the base of the massive tree to the spot where Gilbert pointed. There was a bowl there formed by the roots which was large enough to comfortably accommodate someone's bottom, making for a seat on which to recline. That in itself said nothing in particular, but then about three paces away, by the trunk of a large beech, there was a pile of horse manure, no longer green and fresh, but brown. Stephen knelt by the pile and cut one its balls apart. The interior was green, which meant that it had been deposited not too long ago; it even could be no older than the date of William Griffin's death, although there was no way of proving it.

He stood up and returned to the oak. He could not see the road from this spot, of course, but neither could anyone on the road see him, which made it a likely spot for an ambusher to wait for prey to pass by. It was a good enough hiding place for at least one man, but may not provide enough concealment for more. He returned to the road for a moment for a look back, and decided that was true. The others must have hidden elsewhere. For there had to be at least three attackers, perhaps more. It would have taken at least three men to bring down William Griffin and the groom, for he had no doubt that the arrows that struck them were released simultaneously. Even the fastest shooter could not renock and shoot quickly enough to hit Griffin twice, let alone the groom. Otherwise, one or both of them would have got away. Where had they hidden?

The only answer was deeper into the wood. Stephen stepped a few yards away from the oak to the edge of the road. He then walked into the forest in a half circle with the oak at the center. He found nothing of interest at first and repeated this process, circling deeper into the forest each time, examining the ground with care.

At last, however, his diligence was rewarded. He came upon a place about forty yards in that was greatly disturbed, the leaves shuffled this way and that, and piles of manure.

So the ambush had been simple, as he suspected. A lookout, the one with the bottle, had kept watch on the road, while the others remained within the forest out of sight. The lookout was drinking from his leather bottle when William Griffin and Tad the groom appeared. In his haste, the lookout dropped the bottle as he gave the signal and, when the victims passed, the bandits rushed into the road and shot Griffin and the groom down from behind.

Stephen took a step to get around an elm and something sharp stabbed the heel of his bad left foot. He let out an oath and hopped away.

Gilbert, who had followed Stephen's inspection without comment, bent at the offending spot and came up with an arrowhead that had broken from its shaft. It had the blunt look of a crossbow bolt rather than an arrow proper. It could have been dropped by a hunter but the coincidence of finding it where the horses of the attackers had been tethered strongly suggested that one of them had been armed with a crossbow.

Slipping the arrowhead into his pouch, Stephen returned to the road, where Ralph waited. A short distance beyond Ralph, a fox emerged from the forest and entered the road. It paused, studying the men, and judging them not to be threats at the moment, it trotted across and disappeared.

"Were you here to see what happened?" Stephen murmured to the fox. "What story could you tell me?"

"What have you found?" Ralph asked as Stephen and Gilbert reached him.

Stephen explained briefly, then showed him the bottle. "Have you ever seen anything like this?" he said.

Ralph turned the bottle over in his hands. "I have not."

"You don't recognize that maker's mark?"

Ralph shook his head.

There was one other thing bothering him and it was a moment before he got his hands on it.

"This road," Stephen said. "It's not well traveled."

"Local traffic mostly, yes, sir," Ralph said.

"And not a lot of it, either."

"No, sir. I don't expect so."

"Who at the manor knew that Lord William had gone to Bewdley?"

"Why, everyone, I expect, even the house cats. It wasn't a secret. He went every Saturday."

Chapter 9

It was almost time for the funeral Mass when Stephen and the others returned to Fox Hall Manor. The yard was packed with neighbors. While there might not have been fifty on the nose it was close, all gentry by their multicolored finery, men and women wearing their best, except for a mass of browns and grays and unwashed linen, the people of the village who were relegated to one side behind ropes so they could not mingle with their betters.

They had come too late for the vigil and recitation of the rosary, when mourners viewed the coffins and said prayers for the dead over them. Because there were so many mourners, the Mass was held outside in the open air. The pallbearers, led by Philip Galant, brought the coffins out of the chapel and set them on the ground. Standing at the chapel doorway, the priest, hired from Kidderminster, called for silence in a shrill voice and, when the tumult of voices subsided, he began the Mass. So far at the rear, Stephen and Gilbert could not make out what the priest said, although the sounds were familiar since they had attended funeral Masses before and they were all the same. There was a great deal of comfort in the ritual and the fact it never changed. There was a reading from Scripture, a eulogy, a song of praise, various blessings and prayers, a sprinkling of holy water, and the recitation of more blessings, but, unusually, no offer of Communion, perhaps because there were far too many people.

When the priest finished his work, Galant and the other pallbearers took up the caskets and carried them solemnly around the chapel to the graveyard, where two graves had been dug during the previous night. Additional blessings were bestowed, more holy water expended, and at last, the coffins were lowered on ropes into the ground. Galant provided the first shovels-full of soil on both coffins and then stood back for the villagers to finish the task of covering them.

The crowd proceeded to the house where an enormous funeral dinner had been prepared. Two cows had been slaughtered and roasted, three pigs, and five sheep, and the various dishes concocted from them were served on long tables erected in the hall that, miraculously, held every gentry visitor; there were some disputes about where people should sit based on their degree of friendship with the deceased, but Dyne somehow managed to sort things out so that no one's feelings or pride suffered more than a little. The villagers ate in the yard.

As strangers to the family, Stephen and Gilbert found places near the door, which emitted drafts owing to the fact that the wooden entry screen had been taken down to accommodate all the visitors. But they didn't object. At least they weren't in the yard with the villagers, where it had begun to drizzle; not heavily, but enough to be annoying and chilling.

Afterward, as the servants took down the tables and removed the benches, the serious drinking and socializing started. Although funerals were a dreadful business, they were also an opportunity for people to exchange gossip and for young men and women to do what young people always do when they have such a chance to be together, the girls without their chaperones, and for the mothers to size up their daughters' marriage prospects.

However, before all this could start in earnest, Galant rose to his feet and called for silence. He got it pretty quickly; perhaps those present thought he was going to offer another prayer for the souls of William and John Griffin.

But instead of a prayer, Galant said, "Gentlemen! Ladies! I wish to make an announcement. You all know how dear to me William and John both were, and how grievously I feel their loss. Therefore, and as their closest male relative, I wish to offer a reward of ten pounds for any information that leads to the arrest of the evildoers."

Galant's generosity — for ten pounds was a great sum of money — provoked gasps of surprise, rapidly followed by shouts of approval.

Galant received these shouts with a wave, and the pitch of conversation rose as servants hurried to serve wine Galant had brought from his manor for the occasion.

He came down from the high table and personally gave Stephen a goblet filled with wine. He clapped Stephen on the shoulder. "I've heard that you have a great reputation for catching murderers — that you are both clever and persistent. Let's drink to success." He raised his cup and they drank together.

Galant pivoted toward his seat at the high table but Stephen stopped him with a hand on an arm.

"There is one thing I'm curious about," Stephen said.

Galant nodded expectantly.

"Which of the women here is Ingrede Paddoc?

"None of them. She's not here."

"That seems a bit odd, don't you think?"

"She wouldn't have fit in with our crowd," Galant said. "Such a common girl, really. No proper manners."

"You knew her?"

"William had her here a few weeks ago for a feast when they revealed their engagement. Moreover, I have word from Bewdley that as soon as Richard de Plumton heard of William's death he rode as fast as his horse could carry him to Ingrede to press his suit now that William is out of the way. He was very unhappy with the engagement, as he had a lust for Ingrede himself. So I expect Ingrede has better things to do."

"A man determined to get what he wants," Stephen said.

"Just so," Galant said. "And a woman. Now I must get back to my family."

Stephen snagged another cup for Gilbert, and tapped the clerk on the shoulder. Proffering the cup, which Gilbert accepted with eager eyes, since as a commoner he had expected ale, Stephen said, "Did you bring your writing materials?"

"Of course. I always feel naked without them."

"We've need of them."

"What do you have in mind?"

"I am sparing you from the tedium of having to ask people questions. Instead, you will write down what I learn from my discussions with the guests."

"Don't trust your memory?"

"No more than I trust yours. You'll take notes of what I hear. Perhaps we may learn something useful."

Gilbert clumsily wended his way through the crowd to the stairway leading to the upstairs chambers, where their baggage was stored, to glances of annoyance from some of the mourners that so obvious a commoner as this little fat man would be allowed to knock elbows with them. He returned shortly. Stephen met him at the foot of the stairs to spare him having to repeat his trek through the crowd.

"This way," Stephen said, having to shout to be heard over the din. He led Gilbert to the high table, where Galant was sitting with his wife and two sons.

There was a vacant chair at the far end. Stephen gestured to it. "Do you mind if my clerk shares the table?"

Galant pursed his lips as if he thought to object. But he said, "Feel free."

He watched with some interest while Gilbert unpacked quills, ink bottles and parchments from a leather case and sat down. But then two women approached to say how sorry they were at his cousins' untimely deaths.

"Now what?" Gilbert asked.

Stephen spent the next two hours circulating through the crowd, questioning all who would give him a moment about the robberies and murders that had occurred hereabout. Just about everyone was willing to express an opinion about how terrible the situation was, how unsafe the roads, the disruption in commerce and the privations that caused (especially in the sudden drought in luxury goods), and horror at the mutilations of the dead. Stephen's focus, however, was exactly where any incident happened. People's knowledge, though, was often vague — on the road between Kidderminster and Worcester, on the Bridgnorth road, near Amblecot (wherever that was), beyond Stourbridge, a couple of miles outside

Bromsgrove, and so on and on and on. Some knew the victims and that information tended to be rather better. After every fourth or fifth interview, Stephen struggled through to the high table and recounted to Gilbert what he had learned.

He also asked people about the leather bottle and its maker's mark. Most knew no more than Ralph the hayward. But one lord from a manor near Kidderminster said he knew of a leather worker in the village of Birmingham who used that mark.

"His name is Mansell atte Noke," the lord said. "He does good work. I even have one like that myself. I prize the wax on the leather. Is this about all those murders?"

"I am not sure," Stephen said.

"Ah, well, best of luck with your inquiry."

When Stephen returned for the last time to the high table, he found Gilbert scribbling on a separate piece of parchment than the notes he had taken down. He appeared to be drawing to no purpose.

"Whiling away your time there, eh?" Stephen said.

"I thought I would take a stab at a map." Gilbert turned the parchment around so Stephen could see it.

"I did not take you for an artist," Stephen said. "I thought you only did lettering."

"Well, that's true. But I've always had a fondness for maps."

"When did you ever see a map?" Stephen said. Area maps like Gilbert's were rare things, works of art, for the most part. Most maps made by and for ordinary people consisted of a simple drawing of the route from one place to another, usually town to town, with landmarks noted on the way. Even these were not common; most people unfamiliar with a route just asked for directions from anyone they happened upon.

"Why, at Greater Wenlock, of course. There are many fine maps there. This one I drew from memory. It's from a much better one, I admit. But take a look."

Gilbert had depicted the towns of Bridgnorth, Bewdley, Kidderminster, Stourbridge, Bromsgrove, Wolverhampton, and Worcester as little squares with the name of each town written beside it. Each square was connected by a thread, the line meant to depict a road. Along those lines were small X's.

"Those marks," Gilbert indicated the X's, "are where the murders took place — best as I can determine." He tapped the notes. "Most of what you told me made it rather impossible to know where one happened for certain. So, get ready for it, they're guesses."

"I'll let you get away with that just this once. Here are two more," Stephen said, giving Gilbert what little he had heard, and Gilbert bent over his map to add the appropriate marks before making further notes of what Stephen had said on the other parchment.

"Have you ever thought of making any of those route maps?" Stephen asked as he puzzled over Gilbert's map. "You know the kind I mean. You could sell them to travelers at the inn. It would bring in extra money and they wouldn't cost anything to make."

"Hmm," Gilbert said. "I hadn't thought about it."

"Yes," Stephen said, warming to this idea. "You could make a master for a given route and then recopy it at need. And you could get your information from other travelers. Pick their brains. You know how travelers love to talk. It would cost you nothing."

"I do rather like that idea," Gilbert said.

"Anything to make the inn more profitable," Stephen said.

"What have you done with my noble knight and deputy sheriff? The man standing before me sounds like a simple merchant."

"Don't tell anyone that I suggested it."

"Well, I shall at least have to tell Harry."

Telling Harry anything meant that within moments the entire town of Ludlow would know.

"If you do, I will break all your quills and spill all your ink," Stephen said.

"You are a cruel man."

"As one must be in order not to be taken advantage of. Here, I've done nothing more than offer sound advice and what do you do? Threaten to blacken my reputation."

"Well," Gilbert muttered, "you do enough of that by yourself. You don't need my help."

Sadly, this was true and Stephen did not respond any further.

Meanwhile, Stephen grew dismayed as he examined Gilbert's crude drawing. There were X's all over — on the road from Bridgnorth and Kidderminster, two on the road between Bridgenorth and Cleobury, several about Stourbridge and toward Birmingham, but many more to the east and south, on the roads to Worcester, Birmingham and Bromsgrove. There was no rhyme or reason to any of it.

"It's not very helpful," Stephen said gloomily.

"That's what we get for trusting to gossip."

"We will have to dig deeper."

Chapter 10

"You're determined to see Richard Deme, then," Galant said the next morning as he waited for his horses to be tacked up so he and his family could return to Upper Arley.

"That seems as good a place to start as any," Stephen said. He wasn't sure how much the Staffordshire coroner could help, given the fact that his examination of the bodies had not been thorough, but it was a stone that needed to be turned. There was never an easy way to do any of this.

"You'll need a guide," Galant said. "The way to Stourton twists and turns down many obscure lanes. There is no straight way to get there. Come with us. I'll have one of my grooms show you the way."

"I am obliged to you," Stephen said, glad that he would not have to waste time getting lost, as so often happened when you made your way across England on unfamiliar roads. It usually was not a real journey unless you made at least one wrong turn.

The Galant party led the way on a road north from Fox Hall through a pleasant countryside of gently rolling fields that had already been plowed for spring planting. The soil looked rich and fertile. About a mile from the manor house, the ground sloped downward through pasture where a great herd of cows grazed by the River Severn.

The road swerved left as it approached the river and dipped into a cut, ending at the water's edge.

One of Galant's valets dismounted and removed a red flag from a box by the bank. He waved the flag back and forth over his head until someone on the other side noticed and waved back.

Shortly, there was a flurry of activity on the opposite bank and four men rowed a flat-bottomed ferryboat into the river, pulling hard against the current so as not to be swept downstream. A fifth man steered.

The valets grabbed the bow of the boat as it grounded and steadied it so the Galant family could board. There was only enough room for them and their horses, so Stephen,

Gilbert, the three ladies' maids and four valets had to wait with the baggage.

By rights, Stephen and Gilbert should have been on the next shuttle, but Stephen sent the maids over and then the valets with the pack horses.

By the time the boat returned for Stephen and Gilbert, the rowers were sweating and had shucked their coats.

"Odd place for a ferry," Stephen remarked to the steersman as the boat backed away from the bank and swung about toward the other side. It was indeed an odd place for a ferry. Ferries usually served major roads where there was enough traffic to support the boat and its crew.

"Ah, well," the steersman said. He waved a hand at the pasture on the west bank. "That meadow belongs to Lord Philip, and the cows. His herdsmen need a way to get back and forth to them, and we've got to carry them when we take them to market. But I reckon that we'll be more busy in the days to come."

"Oh?" Stephen said.

"Now that the Griffins are gone, Fox Hall will return to the family," the steersman said, clearing meaning the Galant family.

"It once belonged to the Galants?" Stephen said.

The steersman nodded. "All this once was part of the same manor," he said waving an arm about, indicating the lands on both sides of the river. "Old Lord Percival gave Fox Hall to Lady Alfrida, his daughter, when she married Hugh Griffin. That never sat well with Lord Philip's dad. He thought it should have all come to him, lock, stock and wood lot. But Lord Percival, God rest his soul, had a soft spot for Lady Alfrida." He sighed. "She was a great beauty and could charm the legs off a frog. They'll be missed, the Griffins. Good people. Come on, boys! Pull! We're short of the landing!"

After Stephen and Gilbert had coaxed their horses over the bulwark to solid ground, a sandy beach next to the mouth of a small stream emptying into the Severn, Stephen dug into his purse for farthings for each of the boatmen.

"Ah, sir, you don't have to do that," the steersman said. "You're a guest of the lord."

"It's for getting us across safe and dry," Stephen said. "My friend here can't swim." He put the shards of coin onto one of the plank benches. "Get yourselves a pint, on me."

There was more than an hour's delay while a suitable groom was found to show them the way to Stourton and to get a horse tacked and provisions collected for him. The groom assigned to them was not impressive looking. He was no more than twenty, tall and thin so that his feet hung well below the belly of his nag when he mounted, and had sad eyes. His name was Hob Spindleshanks.

Hob led them down the hill from the manor house to the village where they found a road leading northeast away from the ferry. The road climbed steeply at first and then leveled out a bit as they went by a lone cottage behind a stone wall, likely the abode for a shepherd, for sheep could be seen grazing in an adjacent field. Hob did not talk much when Gilbert, ever garrulous, tried to engage him in conversation. Hob grunted at whatever Gilbert said and looked morose and unhappy.

"Is there something wrong, Hob?" Stephen asked as Gilbert grew visibly exasperated at his failure to draw Hob out.

"No, sir," Hob muttered. "Got a bug in my stomach. Not feeling well."

"Then why were you chosen for this job?"

"I come from Stourton," Hob said. "Visit me mum Christmas and Easter. Know the way like the back of me hand. The other boys, they'd just get lost."

"I'd be unhappy, too, to be summoned from a sickbed for this," Gilbert allowed, glad to know that his charm had not entirely failed.

"Sick bed, yes," Hob said. "If only."

Two-hundred yards after passing the shepherd's house, they came to a smithy. Coals on the forge glowed bright red and orange and the air was filled with the smell of hot iron. The smith looked up at the travelers without missing a stroke upon some metal thing he held in a pair of iron pincers. The smith waved at Hob, who nodded in return. The smith spat, though he was apparently not put out by Hob's lack of courtesy, and returned the metal thing to the coals. His apprentice resumed pumping the bellows.

After about a mile and a half they came to a well-traveled road. Hob turned left onto it.

"The road from Kidderminster to Bridgnorth," Hob said in answer to a question not asked. "Don't worry, we won't be long on it. Turn off's not far."

The Bridgnorth Road rose steadily before them but easy, not precipitously, and not a strain on the horses. They kept to a walking pace for there seemed to be no reason to be in a hurry, although it was eight miles from Upper Arley to Stourton and they had gotten a late start. A forest closed in on both sides of the road. Stephen kept an eye out for trouble, but saw nothing suspicious.

About a mile from the point where they had entered the road, a little lane came in from the left, crossed the road and disappeared on the right. Hob turned as if to say something. His eyes went wide, fear blossomed on his gloomy face. He lashed his nag and it burst into a gallop, disappearing to the left.

Stephen turned his head to see what had panicked Hob. Two men had emerged from the wood. One carried a longbow, the other a crossbow. Both men wore masks. Stephen pushed Gilbert from the saddle. The little round man cried out in protest and landed with a pronounced thud. In the same motion, Stephen dived for the ground. Two arrows hissed through the space he and Gilbert had occupied. Before the attackers could shoot again Stephen had his shield off his back, and he crouched to make himself small so he could fit as much of his body behind it as possible. It was a small shield and it felt as though it gave no more protection than a thimble. He edged over to put himself between the shooters and Gilbert, who uttered hideous gasps as he fought to recover his breath.

The one with the longbow drew an arrow from his belt and began to nock it while the crossbowman cranked on the spindle to reload his weapon. Stephen drew his sword. He hated the notion of daring to rise and surrender what little shelter the shield afforded. But cowering where he was invited becoming a pincushion. So he rose and charged. To his astonishment, the assailants turned and dashed into the woods, apparently not liking their prospects now they had lost the advantage of surprise. Stephen did not follow them. Pursuing a man armed with a bow — let alone two — through a forest was asking to be shot. Stephen had no appetite for that.

He returned to Gilbert, who had managed to sit up, although he breathed no easier.

"Anything broken?" Stephen asked.

Gilbert shook his head. "What happened?" he finally croaked. "Why did you do that?"

"As you know, the roads aren't safe." Stephen explained about the robbers. Gilbert paled and continued struggling to recover his breath. Stephen went to collect the horses, which, unconcerned about the near deaths of their riders, had taken the opportunity of freedom to graze on tufts of grass struggling to survive on the roadside. Horses were always hungry.

"Where's our guide?" Gilbert said as Stephen helped him to his feet.

"Run off," Stephen said. "As I would too, if I was him."

"Do you think he'll come back?"

"Would you? He probably thinks we're filled with arrows."

"But how will we get to Stourton from here? Do you have any idea?"

"Not the slightest."

Chapter 11

Stephen could think of nothing else to do but ride to Kidderminster and ask directions from there. It was out of the way but preferable to wandering down country lanes and ending up in Chester or somewhere else far distant from where they wanted to be.

The ride down the Kidderminster-Bridgnorth road took about an hour and a half. It was nervous going, with much looking about and starting at rustlings in the forests, when they came to them, only to have the alert turn out to be an industrious squirrel or random bird. This was particularly hard on Gilbert, who wasn't used to being ambushed in forests and did not take well to it.

By the time they slouched into Kidderminster, Gilbert's nerves were so frayed that he leaped from his horse at the nearest inn, where he ordered a pitcher of ale and settled himself in a corner to await the coming of a meat pie. Some people drank to sooth their nerves. Gilbert preferred to eat his way to tranquility. Stephen saw to the horses then followed him in, glad there was a meat pie waiting for him as well. He broke the crust of the pie with concealed eagerness; it was pork and peas in a brown sauce and smelled very good.

"Not bad," he said with a full mouth; the contents were so hot that they burned his mouth and talking was as good as breathing to dispel the heat.

"The Shield makes better," said Gilbert sourly, already halfway through his pie.

"Everywhere you go you say the Shield does better."

"You should too. You used to live there and you are a drain on our supplies still."

This was because Stephen owned a quarter of the inn and he and his family took their profits, meager as they were in these hard times, through meals there. He had not guessed until now that the Wistwodes resented the practice.

"My, you are upset," Stephen murmured.

"I'm not used to being nearly killed and thrown off a horse. Nearly killed twice, in fact." Gilbert wiped his mouth on a napkin and waved to a servant for another pie.

"The least you could do is say thank you. If it wasn't for me, you'd be a pincushion."

"Just promise you'll never push me off a horse again. You know how I hate falling off horses."

"I can't imagine why you would. But all right. I promise." Stephen kept his fingers crossed under the table. He never knew what dangers might arise in the future that could require him to do such a thing again. Was it a lie if you said it for someone's good?

Refreshed and reinvigorated, they collected their horses. The innkeeper and the leader of a packhorse train were helpful in providing directions. They both spoke over each other, vying to be the first to give advice. This made sorting it all out a bit difficult, but what they had to say boiled down to: "Take the north road out of the marketplace and then go left where the street forks. Keep on it for two miles and take the road to the right, where there's a big yew growing by the roadside. If you miss it and find yourself in Cookley, you've gone too far. Keep on through Whittington till the road dead ends ('not quite' protested the innkeeper). Turn left and cross the bridge over the River Stour, and you're at the castle."

"A pleasure meeting you, sir," the innkeeper said ingratiatingly as they gathered the reins of their horses. "Will you be coming back this way again? Oh, and I didn't get your name."

"Adam Hocksley," Stephen lied. He wasn't sure if his infamy as one of those who had retaken Ludlow Castle for the king had reached into Worcestershire. But there was no point in taking chances, since the county sheriff was a barons' man. "And this is my valet, Odo."

"A pleasure to make your acquaintance, too, good Odo," the innkeeper said.

As they rode down the street toward the market, Gilbert grumbled, "Odo?"

"It just popped into my head. Anyway, you look like an Odo. It has sort of a learned ring to it, don't you think?"

"But a valet," Gilbert snorted. "You could have done better than that — demoting me to a valet!"

"The fellow surprised me. Besides, you could be a valet. Well, maybe not. You don't look subservient enough. Oh, well."

Richard Deme was a husky man with a square face, a receding hairline and a frown that did not go away. Stephen thought at first that Deme was irritated at his appearance and the interruption it seemed to cause to some more urgent business. But he ultimately concluded that it was just Deme's usual expression.

They sat by the hearth fire in the hall as servants began setting up tables for supper, for Stephen and Gilbert had arrived late in the day. Deme's fingers tapped his knee as he listened to Stephen's explanation of what he was about.

"I was wondering when Alditheley would get around to doing anything about this," Deme said, the frown deepening. Great grooves lengthened on either side of his mouth. "Dreadful business. The roads are not safe in any case, but these murders have just made things worse. People are afraid to go out. Commerce is at a standstill. I haven't been able to buy a decent cask of wine in more than a month."

"What do you know about them?" Stephen asked. "When did they first begin?"

"There were three in my jurisdiction last September. Then nothing until about a month ago, when there were five, not counting the one above Bewdley."

"What makes you think they are related?"

"Well, they're hard to miss. All the victims were shot through with arrows. The faces of the gentry were slashed. Very gruesomely, I might add."

"The gentry but not the commoners?"

Deme nodded. "And all were killed. You know how your usual highway robber works. He and his fellows ambush a group, some of the robbers blocking the way in front, others cutting off retreat. They all have bows, but they rarely shoot. Threats and fear are their weapons. They take what they want, usually money and jewels and whatever else they can easily carry off, and away they go into the forest. I've known victims to be tied up so they couldn't pursue and for the women to be raped first. But I've never seen a case where all the travelers in a group were shot down outright and killed where they lay. Even the women." Deme's voice shook.

"Groups, you say."

"Yes," Deme growled. "Some as large as ten." He shook his head. "You cannot imagine the horror of it."

"We saw what was left of William Griffin," Stephen said.

"Oh, you did, did you? Imagine that multiplied. I've seen a dozen such now." Deme gazed into the fire, his frown growing thunderous.

"Where did the ones last year take place?" Stephen asked.

"Two on the road between Bridgnorth and Kidderminster. One was a mile or so outside Quatt, one off that road toward the ferry at Hampton, and the last not half a mile away on the road to Wolverhampton. The bastards had to have passed by here on the way to and from, but nobody noticed anything untoward," he said grimly.

"And the others?"

"One on the road between Kidderminster and Bridgnorth near Alveley. Two others on Bridgnorth Road by Romsley, and the remaining two in the wood called Four Ashes."

"We have a map. Perhaps you could indicate where these places lie."

Gilbert handed Deme his map. Deme stared at it as if he had never seen anything like it.

"What are these marks?" he said.

"We questioned the people at William Griffin's funeral," Stephen said. "These mark the places where we were told murders similar to Griffin's took place."

"Hmmph," Deme snorted. "There's far too many of them, and they're all wrong in any case."

After some study, he fingered the approximate locations of each of the murders he had investigated. Gilbert marked those places on the map with the letter D.

"I don't see what good that's going to do," Deme said.

"It helps focus one's thoughts," Stephen said. "Do you know anything about similar murders committed out of your hundred?"

"No, there've been none as far as I know, except for one in Offelow Hundred to the east. It was near Oldbury, I think," Deme said. He glanced at Gilbert's map. "I've heard there've been a few in Worcestershire. But that's just gossip. You'll have to ask the authorities there to be sure."

He added, "There is one other unusual thing. The robbers also took all the horses."

"Did they," Stephen said contemplatively. This was unusual. Robbers normally only took what they could carry with them — money, jewelry, food sometimes, random bits deemed valuable and easy to haul off. But they seldom took horses. Perhaps this was because they rarely attacked mounted parties, which were normally well armed and able to defend themselves; cart horses were troublesome to unhitch and a quick getaway was prized.

"Yes," Deme said. "One of them was a fine stallion. I tried to break him myself but could not. Such a beautiful animal; a chestnut with a white star on his forehead and white socks on all his feet. I sold him to the lord of Claverley. A tiresome debt I owed. Claverley was one of those killed on the Bridgnorth Road." He shuddered. "I hate to think of that fine animal in the hands of poltroons. They'll ruin him, as sure as I sit here."

It turned out Deme was misinformed. The additional deaths took place on the road connecting Birmingham and Wolverhampton outside the village of West Bromwich. It was another well-traveled route. The victims were the son of the lord of a manor called Wightwick and two companions on the way to Birmingham for a joust scheduled between the son and another young lord to settle a quarrel between them. According to Stephen's informant in West Bromwich who claimed to have seen the bodies, the victims were shot down with arrows, their faces slashed, and their horses and all their knightly equipment taken. It happened about three weeks ago, the same time as the other killings in Seisdon Hundred.

West Bromfield was only about six miles from Birmingham and since it was hardly noon, there seemed no good reason not to go there and look up the bottle maker to see if he had anything useful to say. Stephen did not have high hopes but it had to be done.

The town rose into view as they came over a slight rise and saw it about two miles away. It was not walled, like so many towns, but had grown haphazardly along a series of streets that wandered away from a large, triangle-shaped marketplace dominated by a small red stone church at its base. To the west of the church stood the manor house, also in red stone, surrounded by a circular moat.

They arrived at the marketplace after descending one street that had to be the hive of tanners. The stench of urine and feces used in the tanning process was so strong here that both Stephen and Gilbert had to cover their faces with handkerchiefs; that did little good, however, and neither could scarcely breathe. Yet the stench, which lay on this part of the town like a sodden blanket, did not seem to bother any of the townspeople. Those folk went about their business as if nothing was the matter. The manor house was within easy range of the tanners and Stephen marveled that the local lord had not run them off to a safe distance. But then the matter probably boiled down to rents; more could be collected on these town burgage plots than at some place farther away. Stephen wished for a breeze but was disappointed.

"I feel sick. I don't think I'll be able to eat a thing today," Gilbert groaned.

"Give it an hour and you'll be fine," Stephen croaked, his voice muffled by his handkerchief.

The search for the bottle maker, Mansell atte Noke, consumed half an hour, but at last they located his shop down a lane east of the market. It wasn't far enough from the tanners that you could no longer smell them, but the odor wasn't choking.

Noke had his shutters down to form a counter, and he and two boys were busy making leather goods at a table inside the shop. The boys cut leather using a pattern while Noke himself applied a stamp to what looked like it would be a belt pouch in order to leave it with a distinctive design. The shelves behind the working men were stocked with different leather goods — pouches, tankards, pitchers, belts, thin leather laces for boots, a leather case for documents, and every other small item you could imagine.

Noke looked up as Stephen and Gilbert dismounted at his window.

"Ah, sir," he said to Stephen. "Can I interest you in something?"

"Information," Stephen said. He drew out the leather bottle from his pouch and set it on the counter. "I'm told that's your mark."

Noke examined the mark.

"It is," he said. "What of it?"

"The bottle's new. I wondered if you remembered who you sold it to. It can't have been that long ago."

Noke considered the bottle for a few moments. He pulled on his lip in thought. "I think I do recall. No more than a week or two ago. It was heavy-set fellow, blond hair, lanky, needing a wash."

"Did you happen to notice anything else about him? Anything that set him off from other folk?"

"Well, he had a scar on his lip." Noke touched the left side of his mouth. "And his nose was crooked and rather flat. Like someone had hit him with a board. He had a hard look about him too, as I think about it. A man not to be trifled

100

with. Although he was well mannered enough when he was here. Oh, and he was dressed rather well. Not as well as you. But he gave the impression of being a man-at-arms. A salaried man. He carried a sword. And a buckler."

"You didn't happen to get his name, did you?"

"No. He asked to see bottles like this one. I set a few samples out for him. He selected this one, paid and left."

"Was he alone?"

Noke frowned. "No … there *was* someone with him."

"Can you tell me anything about him?"

"I'm afraid I can't. The second fellow said nothing and I didn't pay any particular attention to him."

"You know," Gilbert said as they walked back toward the marketplace to find an inn for the night, "that mystery fellow may not be one of our killers."

"What?"

"I mean, what if he's one of the *victims*? And our actual killers lifted his bottle. It is a nice bottle. I'd be tempted to take it if I was in their shoes."

Stephen almost stopped as he considered this notion. "As far as we know, there've been no other killings than that of William Griffin in the last week. He has to be one of them." A man with a split lip and broke nose. It was the first solid lead they had and he wasn't going to let go of it easily.

"But it could have happened during an attack we haven't heard about yet."

"You hungry?" Stephen asked, to change the subject so as not to have to admit he'd failed to consider this alternative.

"I am, a little," confessed Gilbert.

"Well, there's an inn," Stephen pointed across the street. "Let's try there."

Stephen and Gilbert stumbled down the stairs early the next morning for breakfast. The fire in the central hearth had just been kindled and the flames were timid and weak. But even this was better than a moment longer in the chamber they had been allotted. There were no beds in the chamber, only straw-filled pallets, which enabled the innkeeper to put upwards of twenty people in it. The pallets were so closely packed that it was impossible to get out without stepping on someone. It had been hard to sleep as well with all the belching, farting and coughing that had gone on throughout the night. After the third person had trod on Stephen, he had enough. He rose, rolled up his blankets, clutched his gear to his chest, and made his way to the door. Luckily he kept his feet even though he, too, trampled several fellows and a woman on his way.

They had not long huddled by the struggling fire when there was shouting in the marketplace outside. The innkeeper went to the door to see what the ruckus was about and was heard to marvel, "Good God! There's been a gaol break!"

This shocked announcement spurred those about the fire to rush into the street not so much to assist in catching any escapees (who were reckoned to be long gone anyway) as to savor the excitement of such an extraordinary event. Fights, even stabbings (there had been one a week ago in this very inn), were entertaining enough, but an actual gaol break happened only once in a decade or so, and perhaps even only once in a lifetime for most people. Stephen and Gilbert went with the tide.

There was a large crowd gathered in front of the town gaol, a squat wooden building next to the guildhall. Stephen, who was taller than most men, could see over the intervening heads and told Gilbert, who was much shorter, that the door to one of the two cells in the gaol was open and appeared to be empty.

"That's it, then," the innkeeper said, who was nearby. He kicked a clod of dirt in disgust.

"No getting yer money back now, eh, Col?" said a man next to the innkeeper. The tone of voice was cutting, not sympathetic at all.

"Damned right," Col the innkeeper said, ignoring the lack of sympathy. He turned way and headed back to the inn. "All that damage and now I'll not see a penny in compensation."

"I wonder what that was about?" Gilbert said at Stephen's elbow.

"There was a big fight yesterday," said one of the inn's whores who was hopping up and down trying to get a view of the gaol over the heads of the people in front of her. "Lots of damage. Have both cells been emptied?" she asked Stephen.

"No," he said. "Only the one on the left. The other's still locked."

"Oh, happy days," the whore said.

"Could you be more plain in your speech?" Gilbert asked. "You're talking in riddles."

"Jackin Brekebac was in that cell. Him and a couple of others."

"And who is Jackin Brekebac?" Gilbert asked.

"Oh, just one of those wild lads. Comes from down in Worcestershire. Kidderminster way, I think he and his mates said. He started a fight with a gentryman, claimed to have been insulted. They had it out all over the hall. Tables busted, crockery smashed, that sort of thing. Jackin put an end to it finally by clubbing the other fellow over the head with a pitcher."

"Ah," Stephen said. So Jackin would be liable for the damage caused to the inn.

"Why not go after the other party?" Gilbert asked.

"You obviously don't know how things work around here. His dad's a lord. I'm just glad Jackin got away."

"You've a soft spot for Jackin," Stephen said.

The whore flashed a smile. "He's a ruffian, but charming. He makes a girl laugh."

"With a bit of money to spend, too, I expect," Stephen said.

"Well, he had sold a couple or three horses. Came away with quite a lot, if he was to be believed."

"And you did."

"He did spend a pretty penny. More than you'd expect a country lad to have, I'll say that."

"A country lad? That's what he is?"

The girl smiled. "Well, he's a bit more than that. He'd been a soldier in the recent wars. And he talked about it a bit. He served the earl of Warwick and felt he was ill used."

Stephen and Gilbert went closer to the gaol as the crowd broke up. Having broken out of a couple of gaols himself, Stephen had a professional interest in how this had been done. Close up, it wasn't hard to see how. There had been a padlock on the door, but it had been sawn through; just what you'd do if you lacked a skeleton key. Very simple and straightforward and much less noisy than prying off the latch. The accomplices probably waited for the night watch to patrol through the market, and then knowing it would be some time before it returned, set to work. It would not have taken long.

"Stephen, look here," Gilbert said from around the side of the gaol.

He pointed to some hoof prints in the dirt.

"Whoever sprang Jackin likely had horses," Stephen said.

"I won't argue with that guess," Gilbert said. "Speaking of horses, I wonder why a fellow from Worcestershire would come all this way just to sell a few horses."

"Good question," Stephen said. "There are good markets closer at hand, like at Kidderminster and Worcester."

"Insulted by a gentryman," Gilbert mused further, changing the subject in mid-breath.

Stephen nodded. "Slashed faces."

"Someone who carries a grudge against his betters?"

"Seems so."

"Perhaps we should talk to this Jackin fellow," Gilbert said. "It's an unusual name. It shouldn't be that hard to find him. She said he was from Kidderminster."

"Probably a lie."

Gilbert shrugged. "So we will have to sniff about to find him."

Stephen snorted. "That should be no problem. I am a master finder after all. Or so people say."

"How often have I warned you not to put any weight on what people say? You're merely adequate. But how about finding us some breakfast? I'm not sure our inn is up to it after last night's supper. It was wanting."

Chapter 12

"Why so blue?" Joan asked Ida after supper. Joan was nursing a cup of ale across the table from Ida. The children were playing in a corner. Harry let himself down from his seat, crossed to the fire, and added another split of wood to the low flame to keep it going a while longer. Sarah had retreated to the pantry to wash the wooden trenchers, spoons and bowls.

"I am stumped," Ida said. She rested her chin in her hands. "And I cannot think of what to do. Stephen said he intended to question the gate wardens, but he didn't tell me what he thought they might know that would be helpful."

Harry pulled himself back onto his seat beside Joan. "He probably wanted to ask if they'd let anyone in after dark that night. Waste of time, though, if you ask me."

"No one's asking you," Joan said. "But why is it a waste of time?"

"There's two things," Harry pontificated. "First, letting people in after the closing of the gates is against the law. The wardens could get fined if they're caught. So no one's going to confess to anyone, least of all Ida, if she asks them about it."

"But wouldn't they tell Stephen?" Ida asked.

"I doubt it," Harry said.

"I don't know," Joan said. "He might be able to scare a confession out of one of them."

"Maybe. But he's not here," Harry said. "Ida can't intimidate a mouse."

"I'm going to have to work on that," Ida said.

"What's the second thing?" Joan asked.

"The only people the wardens admit after dark is someone they know," Harry said.

"Oh, come on," Joan said. "If the bribe is big enough they'd let in the earl of Arundel."

"All right, maybe," Harry conceded. "But they still wouldn't admit to it. Especially not in this matter. If that somebody turned out to be Red John's killer, they might be held to have some responsibility in his death. Their job is to defend the town, after all. Not good for the livelihood, you know. I sure wouldn't say anything."

"Not everyone's like you," Joan said. "You're one of a kind."

"And that's why you'll never be able to replace me," Harry said.

"So it's not worth the effort to go round and question all of them?" Ida said.

"Likely not," Harry said. "Although a walkabout might do you good even in your delicate condition."

"I wish people would stop treating me like I'm made of glass," Ida said.

"Stephen's concern getting to you?" Harry asked.

"A little," Ida said. But she smiled.

"He is such a worrier," Harry said.

"We've been working on the assumption that Red John's killer isn't from town," Ida said.

"Well," Harry said, "he was a popular fellow, well liked. Had no enemies as far as anyone knows. He never diddled with anyone else's wife, nor stole, nor cheated, wasn't argumentative and given to bluster. Never had a single fight, as far as I know, even with the drunks. So no one in town had a reason to kill him. So, yeah. Some out-of-towner with a grudge seems like the best bet."

"If you were an out-of-towner and you planned to kill Red John, for whatever reason, would you try getting into town after gate closing?" Ida asked. "That seems a risky thing to do. You might not be admitted, and even if you were, you're likely to be remembered."

Joan and Harry nodded together. "Sounds right," they said.

"So if you were the killer you'd come to town the day before," Ida said.

"And you'd find a place to hole up until after dark," Joan said.

"Not an alleyway," Harry said. "Too much chance the night watch might find you."

"Right," Ida said. "That means an inn."

There were only three inns within the walls of Ludlow. The Broken Shield sat across the street from the Attebrooks' townhouse on Bell Lane. Its chief competitor within the town, the Jolly Turtle, lay on Corve Street between the gate and the Beast Market. And there was the Trumpet in Dinham, so small and cheap with so little to recommend it that it could hardly be considered an inn at all.

Ida's first stop the following morning was the Broken Shield. The proprietor, Gilbert's wife Edith, bore a remarkable resemblance to her husband. She was short and round, with a short blunt nose and mousy brown hair pulled back into a bun; no one had ever seen her hair in any other fashion. However, where Gilbert was jovial and friendly more often than not, Edith was no nonsense. Her gray eyes glinted with impatience and not a bit of charity for lazy workers, fools and people trying to take advantage of her, a perennial problem of innkeepers. The inquiry at the Shield yielded no fruit. Edith knew all the customers staying at the inn on the fateful night. They were all regulars she saw often, and there were damned few of them; there would be more if it weren't for the war and the perilous state of the roads. She vented a bit about that. Ida listened to the rant patiently, nodding where nodding was called for, and murmuring agreement.

Where to go next was a toss-up. The Trumpet was to the west near Dinham Gate. The Turtle was just south of Corve Gate. Both were equally far from the townhouse. Harry insisted that he go with her to the Trumpet since he knew the innkeeper there and it was generally considered a disreputable place, a drinking spot for the soldiers of the garrison, a trysting place where unspeakable things happened in plain sight in the hall, and a refuge for the poorer class of traveler whom it was rumored was as often as not a criminal of some kind. Ida was about to protest that she didn't need Harry's protection. But she stayed silent when it occurred to her that he was more concerned about Joan, whose job involved following Ida everywhere while they were in town; ladies never went out without at least one maid, and many wealthy women liked to flaunt their prosperity by surrounding themselves with a flock of maids. So since Harry had a cabinet to finish that morning for an impatient client, Ida and Joan stepped off to the Turtle.

The Turtle's owner was Noll Ifeld. As he came from another part of England, somewhere in the east and north, it was often hard to understand him when he spoke. He was a lanky man who could blow friendly or hard, as the situation required. This seemed to be a characteristic of innkeepers. He greeted Ida in a friendly manner, however, probably because of her status and the fact that Stephen was her husband and everyone stepped carefully about him these days now he was a coroner *and* deputy sheriff. Everybody with any sense wanted to stay on the good side of the law. Ifeld reported nothing different than Edith Wistwode — there had been nothing suspicious about any of his guests Monday and that night. A few packhorse men, a traveling company of musicians and that was about it. No one the least bit sinister and secretive.

"I had been sure it would be the Turtle, being so close to Red John's place. But the Trumpet it is," Ida sighed when she and Joan hit the street, dodging out of the way of a wagon so loaded with firewood that the stack towered above her head. The horses huffed and snorted and the driver's whip cracked encouragement as they pulled it up the hill to the Beast Market; they hardly looked as if they had the strength remaining to make it even that far.

Harry was not finished when they got back to the house and they had to wait two hours. Finally, the impatient client appeared to claim the cabinet. Harry gave Joan the four shillings he received for their savings.

Ida and Joan walked behind Harry's cart down Mill Street to Camp Lane, also known as Mill Lane depending on whom you talked to about it. This was a narrow track that ran along the southern wall of the town.

Ida had never been here before, and she studied the small houses with interest. Some of the poorest residents, mainly weavers and dyers and mill workers, lived here in little thatched houses that were scruffy and seemed in danger of collapse at a sneeze. Ida had seen tents that were bigger. Barefoot children played football in the street despite the cold. The boys — and three girls — stood aside and regarded their disturbers with insolent and resentful eyes.

"Tenney!" Harry barked at one of the older ones, who bent to pick up a stone. "Don't you dare, you little brat!"

Tenney tipped the stone from one hand to another with a speculative, judging look in his eye. "What do you say, mates? Think I can hit a moving target?"

"Ah, go on, he's so close you could piss on him. You can't miss," one boy said.

"Mind your manners," Harry said. "There's ladies present. One's Stephen Attebrook's wife. You don't want him paying your mum a visit, now, do you?"

Tenney fixed an eye on Ida. He pursed his lips, then threw the stone over Harry's head. It struck a thatched roof on the other side of the street and tumbled down, just missing one of the girls.

"Watch it, or I'll fix you!" the girl shouted at Tenney.

She was bigger and older than Tenney but he made an obscene gesture at her and stuck out his tongue.

"You'll have to catch me first," Tenney said.

"That won't be hard," the girl said.

That seemed to be all there was to it, and nothing happened at first as the wagon drew off toward Dinham. One of the boys rolled the football back into the street and the game resumed. Then the girl almost struck by the stone knocked Tenney down in the ensuing scuffle. He landed hard and sat up, holding his head.

"What you do that for, Rose?" he said.

"I felt like it," Rose said.

The game went on.

"Ah, the joys of youth," Harry said over his shoulder. "So sweet, so sublime."

"How do you know Tenney?" Ida asked.

"He and some of his mates used to throw stones at me when I worked Broad Gate," Harry said. "I guess he wanted to pitch another for old times' sake. You know, relive the joy of pelting a cripple."

Ida shivered at the thought of Harry being pelted with stones, but she said nothing.

She was glad when they rounded a bend and Harry pointed out the Trumpet. By a curious twist of geography, it occupied a triangular plot of land where Dinham Lane, running down from the castle, struck Mill Lane as it continued its march along the wall to Dinham Gate in the west. Whereas most houses had their timbers painted black (since it was cheap), the Trumpet's owner had splurged on a festive blue, which was beginning to fade. With this paint scheme and the sign of a prancing jester tooting a trumpet above the door, it could not be mistaken for anything but an inn. Harry had explained that, despite its color, it was a cut-price inn for travelers unable or unwilling to pay the greater fees of better and more comfortable places like the Broken Shield, the Jolly Turtle or the Pidgeon north by the River Corve bridge. The food was also bad. But it was a place where nobody asked where you were from or what was your business.

"They've got two rooms for sleeping, more than you usually find in cheap inns," Harry said. "But they're tiny — about the size of the horse stall I used to sleep in at the Shield — and you have to bring your own bedding. 'Course you can always sleep in the hall. But I wouldn't. The lice and fleas, you know."

"And we have to go in there?" Ida had asked with distaste at the prospect of lice and fleas.

"I suppose I could ask your questions for you," Harry said. "It's probably for the best, anyway."

"No," Ida said, suspecting Harry had brought up lice and fleas to discourage her from going inside. "It's my job. I'll do it."

At their arrival, Harry slipped from the cart while Joan tied the reins to an iron ring fixed to a timber by the door. Harry reached for the latch but Ida beat him to it and opened the door for him. Harry went in. Ida and Joan followed.

The hall was triangular, with six tables arranged about the walls. They were not occupied. To the left were barrels of ale on racks. Anyone asking for wine at such a place was bound to be disappointed. Ida was surprised to see a large fireplace taking up most of the back wall (she longed for one in her own house and felt a vague resentment that such a lowly place had one); it was open so you could see through to the kitchen beyond the wall, so it served double duty, providing warmth and food. The floor was bare dirt, the sort of place that did not favor lice and fleas. They preferred the comforts of the old straw that many people put down upon the dirt. Ida stepped into the hall with less trepidation.

A broad-bottomed woman was cleaning wooden cups in a bucket when they entered. She hung the rag she was using on the edge of the bucket. "Well, Stumpy," she said. "What are you doing here?"

"Don't call him Stumpy," Joan said sharply.

"Who's this?" the broad-bottomed woman asked, not fazed by the rebuke.

"My wife, Joan," Harry said. "I don't believe you've met. And you better watch yourself around her, Abby. She may appear small and harmless, but she's mean as hell."

"Thank you, Harry," Joan said.

"And I am Ida Attebrook," Ida said.

"Oh, yes," Abby said. "I've heard about you. M'lady," she added after a pause. "What brings you to my humble house? I am surprised you'd even be seen within ten yards of us."

"I have some questions to ask you on behalf of my husband," Ida said.

"Is she serious?" Abby asked Harry.

"Deadly serious," Harry said.

"Why can't Sir Steve ask them himself?" Abby said.

"He has been called away on other business," Ida said. "His work falls to me in his absence."

Abby stroked her chin, not altogether believing this outlandish claim. But she said, "Ask away, m'lady."

"It doesn't look like you've had much custom this week," Ida said.

"We've had guests," Abby said in a defensive tone.

"Lots of guests?"

"A few."

"Tell me about them."

"There were a couple of peddlers. Two on pilgrimage. Fellows in a packhorse train." Abby frowned as if it was an effort to remember. "And three fellows whose business I don't know. Hard looking men. Soldiers. I thought they might be with the garrison, or looking for a place there."

"Did they ask you anything about the garrison?" Ida asked.

"No. They weren't very talkative. Although one of them did inquire about the night watch."

"You didn't find that odd?"

"I don't pass judgment on my guests. Their business is their own."

"Yet you must have wondered. It is an odd thing to inquire about, don't you think?" Ida said.

"Well, they did go out after curfew."

"When was this?"

"Monday night."

"How long were they gone?"

"An hour? I don't know. I don't keep track of people's comings and goings," Abby said.

"Is that all you have to say about them?"

Abby shrugged. "When we got up next morning, they were gone."

"Which means they left before dawn," Ida said.

"I reckon so."

"Can you tell me what they looked like?"

"I only got a good look at one of them."

"How is that possible in such a small place as this?" Ida said.

"Some hard men don't like to be stared at. It leads to trouble."

"The one you dealt with — what did he look like?"

"Big and broad, though not tall. About so." Abby held her hand a few inches over her head. "Square jaw, short brown beard, piggish eyes — squinty sort of, you know."

"Did he give himself a name?"

"We don't ask for names around here."

Ida was quiet for a few moments. "Didn't you think any of this was suspicious, given what happened Monday?"

"I can't really say I made a connection. We mind our own affairs here."

"Thank you, Mistress Triplett," Ida said.

"Glad to be of service."

"I am sure you are."

Ida felt a pulse of excitement and satisfaction as the Trumpet's door closed behind her. She had made actual progress, even though it might seem small. She had three people who had acted suspiciously, who had gone out after dark long enough to have made their way to Red John's tavern, killed him and returned. And they had hurriedly left town. And most importantly, she knew what one of them had looked like.

"If you were leaving town at dawn, which gate would you use?" she asked Harry.

"Broad Gate," he said. "No one ever goes out Mill Gate during the night. And Broad Gate's roads lead everywhere you might want to go, to the south, west and east, at least."

"We shall go there."

Reaching Broad Gate by the quickest route, however, meant going back down Mill Lane, where the football game was still underway. They could hear the children's cries and the thump of the ball around the bend. Ida wished to avoid another confrontation between them and Harry. God knew how it would turn out. They had been lucky the first time. So she directed Harry to point his little pony up the steep slope that was Dinham Lane. It was another narrow street where the houses crowded in, giving the impression that they might topple upon them. People said this street was the oldest one in Ludlow and it looked that way.

Somewhere before the top a track between houses and gardens opened on the right. Harry turned into it and stopped.

"My lassie needs a rest," he said. He pointed ahead. "We can cut through here to Bell Lane. No need to wander any higher."

When the pony had recovered her breath, Harry snapped the reins and forward they went; back gardens passed on either side. It was another place that Ida had never been. She thought she knew Ludlow and was discovering that her knowledge was spotty at best. She wondered what else there was to find out about the town.

At length the track emptied into familiar territory, Bell Lane, and they ambled down it to Broad Street and descended to the gate, mindful of potholes and gullies, the perennial hazards of that storied street; they were glad there was no mud to make the journey truly dangerous.

The gate's licensed beggar, Harry's replacement named Wilky, wagged his bowl at them as they arrived. "Come to pay a visit, Harry? Now you're a rich man, how about a small donation."

"I'm short on spare coin today, Wilky. You'll have to wait for another day."

"Stingy bastard, that's what you are." He brightened, though. "What about the mistresses?"

"They're on official business," Harry said. "Don't bother them."

"Official? As in what?"

"As in finding murderers and punishing lawbreakers."

"That's no job for a woman."

"It is today. Now get back. The ladies must have words with the wardens."

"I heard that," said one of the wardens, a scrawny, toothless fellow named Gip as he stepped out of a recess in the passage wall. He was old and bent and looked as though he should be warming himself by the fire while his grandchildren puttered about him. But here he was, still earning an honest wage. (The truth was, he had been disowned by his family, it was said for drink and gambling, and he lived in the gate tower because they didn't want him at home where he was prone to pinch household items for sale to feed his habits.)

Gip bowed elaborately. "Lady Attebrook. How can your humble servant help you?"

"Well, Gip," Ida said, "if you overheard, you know."

"Yes, well, it's got around that you're making inquiries, m'lady," Gip said in a voice heavy with disapproval.

"Yet I trust you will humor me."

"I doubt I have a choice, do I."

"You can answer me, or you can answer Stephen when he returns."

"I suppose," Gip said after a moment.

"I'm glad you see reason. Shall we go inside?"

"Into the tower … with the others?" Gip said. The others being the other men of the guard.

"Unless you want to summon them down so we can have it out here in the street. My questions, however, may require answers that should not be heard by other ears."

"I see, I see," Gip said. "All right, then." He turned toward the recess, which led to a passage upward into the tower, then turned back momentarily. He delivered a kick at Wilky, who slipped out of the way, and growled, "Get back to your place and say nothing about what you just heard, eh?"

Then upward he went with the women trailing immediately behind. Harry followed more slowly.

Broad Gate, which had been built only fifteen years ago, consisted of two drum towers, one on each side of the gateway passage. One of the towers had been rented out as a residence (the aldermen were always anxious to make a profit where they could); the other was inhabited by the six men of the watch. The law required that six men be on duty at the gate at any one time and six were all the aldermen would pay for. So, to ensure there were six men available, they all lived here, even the married ones (although these men enjoyed an upper floor where their abodes were separated by curtains for privacy).

The wardens' chamber occupied the entire first floor. There were framed beds with mattresses, chests for their belongings and pegs upon the walls for hanging weapons, shields and clothing. Two of the men were lying upon their beds, and another was on a bench fiddling with a boot. All rose at the startling sight of women entering their sanctum.

"I'll fetch the others," Gip said, referring to the married men living on the floor above. "You all know Lady Attebrook," he said by way of introduction.

Heads nodded. The men shifted uncomfortably. They could not imagine what Ida was doing here.

"I'll be right back," Gip said and ducked back into the stairway to fetch the married men from the floor above.

Ida and Joan waited awkwardly for Gip to return.

"Oh, hello, Harry," said one of the guardsmen. Seeing Harry, who had managed to make it up the cramped staircase in the meantime, in the guardroom was as startling as seeing Ida and Joan. Everyone seemed reluctant to address Ida. "What you're doing here?"

"Me, nothing in particular. The lady's here to ask questions about Red John's murder," said Harry.

Gip returned at length with the other two men.

Ida cleared her voice. "As Harry says, I've a few questions that have to do with the death of Red John," she said.

"Begging her pardon, m'lady," one of the guards said, "but we don't know anything about that. We were all here on duty Monday night, as always."

"Nobody went near the Blue Duck," another said.

"I am sure none of you did," Ida said. "This is not about that. We know that three suspicious men having the look of soldiers left town Tuesday morning shortly before dawn. We have reason to believe they left through this gate. So my question is, who among you let them out?"

The men stood silently. They shifted again uncomfortably.

"We're all mindful of our duty," a guardsman said finally.

"I am sure you are," Ida said. "Yet the whole town knows that you let people in and out after closing. My husband is often among them."

"Well, he's a special case," Gip said. "Owing to his position and all."

"I suppose he is," Ida said, giving them as stern an eye as she could manage. It did not seem to have any effect. "This inquiry is important to giving Red John justice, as much as we are able." She paused. No one said anything. "I will keep your secret as much as I can. I will only tell Stephen, and my friends and I will not mention it to anyone else. Now, tell me, did three such men leave town before dawn Tuesday?"

"Harry," one of the men said, as if in an appeal to a higher authority.

"You have to talk, Randel," Harry said. "You know me and my wife. And of course Lady Attebrook and Stephen. You can trust us."

Randel rubbed sweaty palms on his coat front. After a long interval, he said, "I let them out."

Randel had the last watch of the night. It was his favorite watch and he was always glad when it fell to him. For one thing, he got a full night of sleep and didn't have to endure being awakened in the middle and then having to struggle to fall back to sleep, which sometimes eluded him. For another, he liked to spend it on the top of the tower in good weather where he had a fine view of town and countryside. The nearly full moon, lacking only a sliver at one edge, was sinking in the west, obscured occasionally by wandering clouds. It was a time when all things were quiet and peaceful.

He paced around the top of the tower taking in the sights of Lower Broad Street, the Ludford Bridge and the river, its rivulets sparkling with the moonshine. Down by Old Street he spotted someone moving in a back garden. A lover slinking away from a secret rendezvous? He wished he could have such an assignation but sadly he was only able to find release with the whores of the Wobbley Kettle once a month when he had saved up enough of his wages.

When he paced around to the town side, he heard voices below. He looked over the parapet. Three men on horses came out of Mill Lane and turned into the gate passage.

There was no doubt what they wanted.

Randel debated what to do. By law he should ignore them when they knocked. But then, a little extra spending money would shorten the time he had to wait to visit the Kettle. The others did it, why shouldn't he?

He made for the stairs and hurried down. The knocking began before he reached the doorway. He opened the door. It was so dark within the passage that he could barely make anything out; only the black outlines of figures at the threshold, their dark horses behind them.

"You want out?" he said.

"Right," one of the men said. He had a deep voice.

"It'll cost you."

"That's not a surprise," the man said. "How much?"

"Halfpenny apiece," Randel said.

"That's robbery," the man said.

"It's late. You woke me up," Randel said.

"Pay him and let's get on," one of the others said impatiently.

"Right, sir," the first man said.

There was a Crooked Man

As that first man fiddled with his purse, Randel stepped out and unlocked the small, man-sized door in the greater gate door. He held out his hand. The man with the money set three halfpennies on his palm. The man's arm was illuminated by the moonlight falling upon Lower Broad Street on the other side of the gate. There was something odd about that arm. The hairiness of the exposed forearm, the sleeve having ridden back toward the elbow as he extended his hand, was one thing, but the more startling aspect was its crookedness, as if it had been broken and not set properly.

"Is there a problem?" the man asked with menace.

"No, no problem," Randel said. He backed out of the way.

The three men trooped through the door, leading their horses, and Randel closed it behind them.

"And you never saw their faces?" Ida asked when Randel finished his tale.

"No, m'lady," Randel said. "It was too dark. And their hoods were up."

This was disappointing. Ida had hoped Randel might confirm that one of the three had squinty eyes and a short brown beard. But she had to go with what he gave her. Perhaps it would mean something in the end. "And what arm was that? The crooked one?"

"The left, m'lady," Randel said.

Ida thought she had learned all she could. Then another question occurred to her. She could imagine Stephen asking it of her and she didn't want to lack for an answer. "Where, exactly, was it crooked?"

"Here, about." Randel indicated a spot six inches from the wrist.

"A busted arm. Well, that's not much," Joan said.

Chapter 13

They were an hour out of Birmingham when Stephen's gut gurgled ominously — ominously because he had experienced something similar that was unpleasant and even life-threatening years ago in Spain. He rode on without saying anything to Gilbert. Perhaps it was nothing; he hoped it was nothing.

But half an hour later, he had to leap from his horse and dash into a field beside the road.

"Is something wrong?" Gilbert called, peering over the hedge.

"A stomach flux, I think," Stephen said, not wanting to share the details of his embarrassing predicament.

The journey to Kidderminster thus proceeded more slowly than usual. There were many halts so Stephen could tend to his bowels, so it was almost dark by the time they arrived.

They entered the marketplace with Stephen bent over his saddle pommel, his stomach feeling as if it was a rag being twisted without mercy.

They dismounted at the first inn they came to. Stephen staggered inside while Gilbert attended to the horses.

"I need a chamber for two," Stephen grunted to the proprietor. "And where's the privy?"

Stephen was sick for three days. When word got around, as it inevitably did, that he had a stomach flux, the inn's proprietor attempted to evict them, but was too afraid to go into the chamber to carry out his order for fear of catching the flux. So he agreed to let them remain if Stephen never left the chamber and they hired an herbalist to burn herbs which he swore would cleanse it of the noxious vapors thought to cause the flux. The herbs stank up the chamber so that Stephen and Gilbert could barely breathe. The herbalist left some of the dried herbs with instructions that some be burnt at least once a day.

"I never imagined that dried cow patties had medicinal properties," Gilbert gasped in distress.

"Is that what it was?" Stephen whispered through the blanket over his head.

"That's what it looked like."

"Must have been an expensive cow."

Gilbert found the choking stench so bad that he sought refuge in the hall below. Stephen had no choice but to stay there and suffer.

There were twenty-seven inns, taverns and ale houses in Kidderminster and over the three days that Stephen was confined and ill, Gilbert visited every one of them.

He came back from the last one as the sun was setting Wednesday evening to find Stephen in the hall, sipping soup from a bowl. There were others in the hall but they had given Stephen a lot of space in case he still exuded vapors of the disease that laid him up.

"Are you sure you should be up?" Gilbert asked anxiously. "And eating something?"

"I think I'm past the worst of it," Stephen said. He set down the bowl. "It's pork, I think. You should try some."

"I am famished," Gilbert said. He waved to a servant and ordered the soup and bread.

"Have you been enjoying your stay in Kidderminster?" Stephen asked.

"I haven't been idle, if that's what you're implying. While you've been loitering about on your back I've found Jackin Brekebac," Gilbert said.

Stephen's soup bowl paused on its way to his mouth. "Really?"

"There's a tavern that he frequents every Sunday with a party of friends," Gilbert said.

"They know him by that name?"

"So they say. He and his friends spend a lot of money there drinking, gambling and whoring. The proprietor said they only started coming so regularly last autumn and they have more money than most country rustics. They didn't come last Sunday."

"Too busy in Birmingham," Stephen said. "Did you learn where they're from?"

"A manor called Harvington. It's about four miles from here on the road to Bromsgrove."

"I have no idea where that is."

"To the Southeast."

"You have been thorough," Stephen said.

Gilbert looked content. "Are you well enough to ride for Stafford and tell Alditheley?"

"I don't think we know enough yet to ask the sheriff to arrest this Brekebac. There could be an innocent explanation for his having money and horses. Perhaps he's selling them for his lord and being well compensated for it."

"Come now," Gilbert said. "There's enough, surely."

"Look who is jumping to conclusions now!" Stephen said.

"I do not jump. I reach my conclusions soberly and after serious reflection."

"Well, I am not convinced. I'm not going to provoke Alditheley to mount a raid on this manor and turn out to be wrong."

"You and your pride. So what do you intend to do now?"

"Pay a visit to Harvington."

"You're going to ride in there and call out, 'where are those robbers I've heard so much about'?"

"Not quite. But something like that."

"It's a mad idea! What if they *are* the killers?"

"I'll just have to take the chance."

Once he was convinced that he would not die from talking to Stephen, the innkeeper was a font of information about Harvington and the surrounding countryside. It was, like much of the land in east Worcestershire, within the forest of Feckenham, which meant the manor's fields were surrounded by woodland held by the king. It lay out of the way, half mile north of the main road connecting Kidderminster and Bromsgrove, which meant that Stephen had to have some special reason for being there if he approached from the south; he could not just claim to be passing through along that road at least. But there was a way he might finesse his story, since a minor track came down from Birmingham from the northeast and passed through the village. The track was little traveled, but it was his only hope of getting into the village without arousing suspicion.

"I beg you to reconsider," Gilbert said. "This is too dangerous."

"I'll be fine," Stephen said.

He dismounted and removed his arrow case and bow from the packhorse as well as a cloth satchel carrying a rolled-up cloak and blanket, a traveler's essentials. He adjusted his peasant's floppy hat and wiggled his shoulders in his shabby peasant's coat. Only a sword and buckler distinguished him from the ordinary rustic.

They were two miles out of Kidderminster on the Bromsgrove road. The area was deep in the forest, some trees almost as big around as a castle tower and scores of feet high, their naked branches a dark tracery overhead.

"I'll see you in a day or two, I imagine," he said.

"If all goes well," Gilbert muttered.

Without any further good-bye, Stephen stepped into the forest. In only a few strides he was out of sight of the road. He heard Gilbert leading the horses back toward Kidderminster, but soon even the gentle clap of hooves was lost as he pushed further ahead. It wasn't long before he came to a small stream. It flowed westward toward its meeting with the River Stour miles away. He turned right and followed it upstream. He moved slowly, stopping and listening often. Since this was a royal forest, there was always the danger that forest wardens, whose duty was to uphold the forest law and prevent trespassing and poaching (all trespassers were assumed to be poachers), and he could not afford to be caught by one of their patrols. The best he could hope for was a prompt beating, an arrest and a sojourn in the local forest gaol. The foresters would never believe any claim that he was on a secret mission for the sheriff of Staffordshire and Shropshire. A gentryman passing as a peasant was too outlandish a thing to take seriously. It was not unthinkable that he could face an immediate hanging. Forest justice was quick and merciless.

He had been following the stream for about three-quarters of an hour when he heard voices ahead. He dived behind a fallen tree trunk covered in moss, his nose filling with the musty odor of decaying leaves. Whoever it was moved without care so at first Stephen thought they had to be foresters, for no sensible person would walk so incautiously in the king's forest. Stephen peeped around the trunk and saw it was two peasants armed with bows, carrying a dead stag on a pole. They had to be poachers.

Stephen waited until he could no longer hear them before rising to continue. He wondered if he had gone far enough north to be above the village and should think of striking out for the lane that descended from Birmingham. He considered following the two poachers to see where they were going. It seemed likely they were heading to Harvington. If he pushed east after them, he was sure to hit the edge of the forest, and that would give him some idea where he was. Yet he was reluctant to do so. What if they stopped for a rest and he blundered upon them? There was no good explanation why he was in these woods and that would ruin what he had set out to do. So he kept on following the stream northward.

After about half a mile, however, the stream crossed a lane running roughly west to east; or rather a lane crossed the stream at a ford. According to what Gilbert had learned in Kidderminster, Harvington was only a mile from the Brompton Road, so he figured he must be north of it. There seemed no reason for this lane to exist if it didn't run into the

Birmingham road. So he turned right upon it. If he happened upon a forest warden, he didn't have to explain his presence.

After climbing up a small rise, the forest gave way to open fields and after about a mile, he came up to a small village consisting of four tumbledown houses. There he found another lane leading southward. This had to be the Birmingham road. There was no one about to ask directions, but that was just as well. This place was close to Harvington and the people here probably went to church in Harvington. It was Thursday. If he had to stay till Sunday, one of these villagers might say something to one of the people of Harvington that could give him away.

He turned upon the track and in a few furlongs saw a flock of sheep grazing in a field to the left. A shepherd was nearby keeping an eye on them with his dog while he played a flute. Stephen and the shepherd exchanged waves. Such a friendly gesture was hardly conducive to the belief that Harvington, if this was Harvington, was a den of thieves and murderers. Half a mile afterward came a village of low, thatch-roof houses surrounded by wicker fences enclosing gardens in which the weeds had been cut and the soil turned in preparation for planting. Washing draped from a few of the fences to dry. In the distance smoke billowed from a forge where the sound of hammering on hot iron could be heard. There was a large paddock containing a dozen horses grazing on piles of hay. By now it was late in the day and the sun hung low, throwing long shadows. The air was chilly.

At the junction of a lane coming in from the left stood a large sycamore that must provide substantial shade in summer but was still bare. A cottage lay within the tree's future shadow. There was a broom hanging above the door, indicating it was an alehouse, and if that wasn't enough to announce its business, there were four tables with benches arrayed in the yard. Two tables were filled with men and women who had knocked off work to enjoy some drink and company before retiring home for supper and bed.

Stephen pushed through the gate. Conversation died as he settled at a vacant table. Those already in the yard looked him over with an exaggerated lack of interest and then looked away. Conversation resumed. He signaled to a serving girl for a pitcher, which she brought after some delay; she deposited a clay cup on the table with a thunk and lowered the pitcher rather more gently.

"That'll be a farthing," the girl said.

Stephen fished out a farthing and surrendered it. The girl went over to one of the other occupied tables, where she exchanged a laugh with a broad-shouldered fellow whose yellow hair hung to his shoulders. A red beard covered his handsome face and his gray eyes danced as he looked at the girl. He patted her on the rear, and the woman next to him punched him in the shoulders. The others laughed. Stephen recognized that man; he was one of the poachers he's seen earlier in the forest. He looked into his cup, determined not to be seen paying attention. He wondered what had happened to the deer. It was advisable to gut it as early as possible to avoid it going gamey; it had been whole when this fellow and his companion carried it by Stephen's hiding place, probably because gutting took time and they wanted to be away from the kill site as quickly as possible to avoid detection.

If Stephen wanted to avoid giving the impression he was watching, it seemed to have failed. The yellow-haired man rose and sauntered over to him.

"We don't get many strangers here," he said.

"Just passing through," Stephen said.

"Where to?"

"Worcester, I think."

The yellow-haired man's eyes traveled over Stephen's bow, sword and buckler. He settled on the bench on the other side of the table. "You a soldier?"

"I try to be."

"Out of work, then?"

"For the time being," Stephen said. "I heard there might be opportunities in Worcester." Stephen waved at the street passing through the village. "I was told that leads to Worcester. Is that true?"

"Stay on it three miles or so and you'll come to a road that will take you there."

"Much obliged."

"Where're you coming from?"

"Chester, originally," Stephen said.

The yellow-haired man snorted. "We're kind of out of the way if you're headed to Worcester."

"I came through Wolverhampton."

"You heard there was work for your sort there?"

Stephen shrugged. He poured himself another cup of ale and raised the pitcher. The yellow-haired man raised his cup and Stephen filled it.

"I was misinformed," Stephen said.

"Why'd you leave Chester?"

"I ran into a spot of trouble."

"What sort of trouble."

"There was a fellow I never got along with. We had words."

"Just words?"

"Well, daggers were drawn."

"A common story."

"And a sad one."

"For you? Because you had to leave?"

"It was for my health," Stephen said.

"I hope the other fellow's all right."

Stephen shrugged again.

"Better not to talk about it, eh?" Yellow-hair said.

"I'm not one to brag," Stephen said.

Yellow-hair nodded. "It's like that, I see."

Stephen did not respond. "The ale's good here."

"It's drinkable. Wolverhampton, you say. Did you happen to pass through Birmingham?"

"I did."

"Anything happening there?"

"How do you mean?" Stephen asked.

"Anything unusual? Out of the ordinary?"

"Not so far as I heard. I was there less than a day. Slept outside town in a barn and just passed through."

"Ah." Yellow-hair swirled the contents of his cup. "How much money you got there?"

Stephen lay one arm on the table; the other was in his lap near the handle of his dagger. "Why? You thinking of taking it?"

Yellow-hair smiled. "Nah. I was thinking of winning it — if you're a betting man."

"Depends on the game."

"How good are you with horses?"

"I've ridden a bit. Why?"

"I've a horse I'll bet you can't ride."

"Do you?" Stephens said.

"He bounces everyone off," Yellow-hair said. "Nobody can stay on him."

"So you can't break him."

"Nobody's been able to."

"I don't know."

"Come on. Tell you what. Keep whatever's in your purse. I'll bet you two shillings against that sword of yours."

"Where did you get two shillings?"

"I'm a careful saver."

"My sword's worth more than that."

"If you had to leave Chester in a hurry and are on the road, you need the money."

Stephen sighed, pretending that what Yellow-hair said was true.

"All right," he said. "I'll take that bet."

Yellow-hair reached across the table. "Done. My name's Jackin Brekebac."

Stephen took the proffered hand. He had begun to wonder if this wasn't Brekebac but he was still surprised to find out it was. "Adam Hocksley."

"That's not your real name."

"No. It's not."

One of the women brought out a small chest from a nearby house and set it on Stephen's table. She opened the lid.

"More than two shillings," Brekebac said. "Want to count it?"

Stephen stirred the little silver pennies, all bright and shiny, with a forefinger. "No. I'll take your word for it. Where's this horse?"

"Over there." Brekebac pointed in the direction of the paddock Stephen had passed coming in.

"Now? Or tomorrow?" Stephen said.

"Now, I expect. There's almost an hour of daylight left. Plenty of time for you to fall off."

"So I get only one try?"

"One try."

"Fair enough."

"I'll be right back," Brekebac said.

He went to the paddock and returned with a chestnut stallion on a halter and leading rein. Stephen inspected the stallion. He was fit and muscular, his lines sleek, his legs firm and proper. He was a beautiful animal and showed his spirit by pulling at the rope and refusing to stand still. There was a white star on his forehead and his white socks on all his legs.

"Does he have a name?" Stephen said.

"We call him the Beast," Brekebac said.

"An ugly name for such a beautiful animal. You know he's worth a fortune."

"Not if no one can ride him."

"Someone will pay a pretty penny for the chance to break him."

"I like him," Brekebac said. "He reminds me of myself."

"Here, then?" Stephen indicated the road in front of the alehouse.

"It's as good a place as any."

Stephen threw the end of the rope over the horse's neck and tied it to the halter, creating a set of reins. He led the stallion through the gate.

"Bring one of the benches," he said over his shoulder.

Two of the village men brought out a bench and set it down.

Stephen urged the stallion close to the bench with gentle flicks of his fingers against the reins where it joined the halter. He climbed upon the bench, gathered the reins in one hand and grasped a handful of mane with the other. There was no saddle so he would have to ride bareback. Stephen had broken horses in Spain and he did not think it was proper and good just to jump on a difficult horse. He liked to accustom a horse to the saddle and then to put more weight upon his back, provided by stacks of grain, and then to work him in the round pen by running him in circles until he realized that bucking brought no relief or reward. But he did not have that choice here. He slipped one leg over the horse's back and mounted before the stallion could shy away.

For a moment, the stallion stood still, as if disbelieving that anyone would dare to ride him. Then, he arched his back and leaped into the air, all four feet leaving the ground and his rear legs kicking outward with such violence and such speed and power that those nearby dove out of the way. He whirled and sent the bench flying, knocking down several spectators — somehow word of the event had gotten out and it seemed that the entire village was here lining the street. As the stallion dashed about, bucking and whirling, people fell back in panic to avoid his terrifying hooves. Stephen held the reins loosely, taking great pains to sit up straight to keep his weight back and his butt on the horse's back as much as he could. If one of the animal's great bounds knocked him either forward on the neck or backward on the haunches, there was no way to stay on.

One way to handle bucking was to ride it out until the horse got tired and concluded that he couldn't knock you off. But this stallion had tremendous stamina. He bucked one way up the street, whirled and bucked back, huffing and snorting, until at last he came to a wicker fence, which he jumped and continued in someone's yard and garden, to shouts of dismay and protest from the owner.

The stallion kept this up for what seemed like forever, demolishing the garden owner's hard work, until he finally came head on with a large woodpile at the rear of the garden that was too high for him to leap and stretched the full length of the yard. He stopped, sides heaving like overworked bellows. He turned his head to look at Stephen, as if saying to himself, should I give more? When Stephen was satisfied that the horse was exhausted, he pulled the left rein and pressed his right foot to the horse's right shoulder to turn him around. They walked back to the front gate. Stephen slipped off and led the horse through the gate.

He handed the lead rope to Brekebac, who accepted it with a scowl. There were scattered cheers but they quickly petered out.

"I'll have my shillings now," Stephen said.

Chapter 14

Stephen earned some good will by paying the garden owner, old Larkin, for the damage out of his winnings. This resulted in his not having to pay for any further drinks, a meal, and a place to stay the night under a roof. All were welcome, especially the supper and the bed, for it meant he would not have to sleep rough on the ground. Even a moldy, scratchy straw mattress could be preferable to the stone and roots of the cold, hard ground. Peasant houses were comfortable in the winter with the fire going and all the drafts patched up.

The drinking went on for many until after sundown, when the western clouds were painted with orange.

Stephen's host for the night, Larkin, patted his shoulder. "I'm retiring now," he said. "My old bones can't take this late-night carousing." He was an elderly man, thin and bent with age who shuffled when he walked. Lanky white hair flowed down about his head from a black woolen cap. "Come when you're ready. No need to knock."

Stephen tossed back the remains of his ale and stood. "I'll come with you. I want to get an early start."

As he and old Larkin crossed the alehouse yard, Stephen was conscious of eyes upon his back. Unfriendly eyes. After the game with the stallion and the pay off, Jackin had taken a seat at one of the far benches. He was joined by four other men who did not look happy with the outcome. They engaged in heated exchanges with Jackin who appeared to shrug off their concerns, acting as if the loss of the two shillings was nothing when in fact it reflected a common man's wages for a month. Stephen could not hear what they were saying. Now and then, one of their number threw a surreptitious glare in his direction.

"Who are those men with Jackin?" Stephen asked as they reached the road and turned toward Larkin's house.

Larkin looked back to see who he meant. He scowled with disapproval. "That's Pate, Randel, Roll and Stace. A good lot gone rotten, I'm sorry to say."

"Troublemakers?"

Larkin opened his front gate. "Times have changed. Once they were just high-spirited. Trouble, but never anything truly serious or that people minded."

"Like hunting in the forest."

Larkin smiled without humor. "What makes you think they did that?"

"Because everybody does, who thinks he can get away with it."

"Done a bit yourself, then?"

"Some. And now? What kind of trouble do they brew?"

"I'll not speak about it," Larkin said darkly. He opened the door to his house, pushed a goat out of the way and entered.

Stephen followed him in.

Sometime later there was a knock on the back door. Whoever knocked did not wait for Larkin to stumble out of bed to answer it. The door creaked open and there was the whisper of feet upon dirt floor.

"Da?" a woman's voice said. Stephen recognized it as belonging to the serving girl at the alehouse, Molle.

"Molle!" Larkin's wheezy voice came out of his dark corner. "What are you doing here? It's so late."

"It's not that late, Da, only a couple hours after sundown." Molle groped her way to the hearth fire where she found a rush light and lit it on the coals. She spotted Stephen, wrapped in his traveling cloak by the far wall. "There you are."

"I've got to talk fast," Molle went on. "You need to get out of here right away. Jackin and the boys are coming for you."

"Now?" Stephen threw off the cloak and leaped to his feet in alarm.

"Not yet. But soon. They're at Jackin's house nerving themselves up and making a plan. They're a little afraid of you, with that great sword of yours and all, worried that one of them might get hurt."

Stephen started to collect his gear. "They mean to kill me? Why?"

"Those two shillings you won, they weren't Jackin's to bet. They belonged to all of them, and the others are angry that you've taken them."

"Where did they get those shillings?" Stephen asked carefully. "Have they been doing robberies?"

Molle looked grim; her young face seemed much lined and older in the rush's dim light. She nodded.

"They weren't always bad!" she burst out. "They were driven to it!"

"Aren't men always?" Stephen said.

"It's true," Molle said. "They were good men once. The war's ruined them."

"It happens to many," Stephen said. "What's their story?"

"They went with Lord William when the earl of Warwick called up his array," Larkin said. "They fought at the siege of Warwick Castle last spring. When the barons' men succeeded in battering down one of the caste's walls, Lord William and the earl ordered them to fight to the last man while they fled to the tower. Jackin and Randel's brothers were killed."

"Yet they managed to survive?" Stephen said.

"They surrendered. Against orders," Larkin said. "Luckily they were spared. But then we are people of no account. Not worth the expense of ransoming."

"How does that turn men to robbery?" Stephen asked.

"Lord William and the earl eventually surrendered," Molle said. "They've been held for ransom — nineteen-hundred marks for the earl and another eight-hundred for Lord William."

Stephen remembered now. John Giffard and Henry de Montfort had attacked Warwick Castle and taken it in April last year. William Beauchamp, the earl, was still in hold as far as he knew.

"Who's Lord William?" Stephen asked

"He holds this manor from the earl of Warwick," Larkin said. "We belong to him."

"The earl and Lord William have squeezed us hard to raise the ransom," Molle said. "People here couldn't pay what was demanded. Jackin and Pate and the others came up with a plan to save us."

"Which was robbery," Stephen said.

Molle nodded again. "They've raised all that was required, but they've got greedy."

"They kept at it when they don't have to," Stephen said.

"Yes," she said heavily. "And now they're coming for you."

"Why are telling me this?" Stephen asked.

"You were good to Da. He's my grand-da," she said. "Most men wouldn't have paid for the damage."

Stephen and Molle left by the back door. Molle led him to the best way to cross the wicker fence, a spot where it met the wood pile, which could be used for steps. She went off into the dark, disappearing before Stephen even made it over. Her stealthy footfalls diminished until there were no sounds but that of the breeze stirring the grass and the thatched roofs.

Left was south, toward what Jackin told him was the road leading to Worcester, which no doubt crossed the same one he had ridden the day before on the way from Kidderminster. He ought to head that way without any more delay but a daring thought popped into his mind and refused to go away. He turned right toward the horses' paddock. It was downwind so the horses were not spooked by his unfamiliar smell, and he approached quietly and slowly so that when the herd became aware of him, they did not startle and whinny.

Stephen slipped around to the gate and took a halter from a post, then he searched slowly among the herd for the stallion. Light from a half moon made it easy to spot the chestnut among the others. The stallion threw his head when Stephen first sought to put the halter on, but settled down to pats and soothing words and finally allowed Stephen to cinch the halter.

He led the stallion out of the paddock and around to the field behind the houses. The smart thing was to lead the stallion away; it was unlikely to rebel at this. But Stephen was impatient now to be gone and the truth was, he found riding the stallion exhilarating. He secured the free end of the halter lead to the halter as he had before to create a rein. Then, grasping the mane, with a leap he swung a leg over the horse's back. It shied away but he managed to keep from falling off, and mounted fully. The stallion shivered and arched his back in preparation for a buck, but Stephen, anticipating his, tugged on the left rein to turn the horse's head, forcing him into a circle, which forestalled it. After making several circles, the stallion calmed down and seemed to accept the situation. Stephen pointed him upon a path bordering the field and asked for a walk. He was afraid to ask for anything more energetic yet. The stallion's spine cut his bottom like a knife, anyway, and would be torture at any faster pace. He hoped that the theft of the horse might explain why he vanished in the night; not because of a warning from Molle.

The village houses slid by on the left; like most villages all of them ran along both sides of a single street. Soon Stephen came to the last house and turned onto the road. Calling it a road was generous; it was really a cart track here as it was north of the village, three strips worn into the turf, two for wheels and one for the horse in the center.

Stephen listened for any sounds of pursuit. But he heard only the wind. An owl hooted; such a mournful lament. A shooting star sprang forth to the north, flaring with a fiery tail that quickly winked out.

The track crossed a substantial road about a half mile from Harvington. This had to be the road connecting Kidderminster and Bromsgrove, the same road he and Gilbert descended yesterday. He turned right and went about a mile before entering a field. He tied the stallion to a hawthorn bush in case it thought of fending for itself while he made his bed. Then he tied the lead rope about a wrist and covered himself with his cloak, using his blanket as a sleeping pad. The stallion was free to graze, and now and again Stephen felt him pull at the rope while he sought the gnarly early grass. But even this occasional disturbance wasn't enough to keep Stephen from a deep slumber.

Stephen woke up to a world so shrouded in fog that he could hardly see the road from where he lay. The horse was standing over him. It had grazed all the grass in a circle about him.

"Thanks for not stepping on me," Stephen grunted as he stood up, draping the cloak over his shoulders against the morning chill. The grass was wet with dew and droplets hung on the hawthorn.

The stallion did not reply. Stephen tied the lead rope to a stick which he drove into the ground some distance from his camp to tempt the stallion to graze some more while Stephen packed up his few things, mainly requiring the rolling and tying of the blanket and stuffing it in his sack.

After that, he held his breath as he mounted the stallion, reaching an upright seat without provoking any resistance.

He headed out to the road and in the direction, he hoped, of Kidderminster.

The fog held all the way to Kidderminster. Despite the weather and the early hour, as it was just after dawn, the town was coming alive with the bustle of commerce. Everything looked different in the fog and he took two wrong turns before reaching the market, and then had to pause and look around for the inn.

He put up the stallion in the stables and went into the hall. Gilbert, not surprisingly, was seated in a corner carving up a small round of bacon.

"Well, you're back early — and in one piece! How did it go?" Gilbert said as Stephen took a seat opposite him. He handed Stephen a cut of the bacon which Stephen bit into with gusto. It was good bacon even if cold and he finished his portion before answering.

"It's them, all right." Stephen told Gilbert about finding the stallion that Deme had described, his encounter with Jackin and his conversation with Molle and Larkin.

"You're sure it's them?" Gilbert asked. "What those villagers told you could prove that Jackin is the one we're looking for. But if put to the question, would they confirm it? After all, every one of them is part of the conspiracy in the end. Now, that horse is powerful evidence by himself if he is the one. But still, it's conjecture until he's identified. So, now what?"

"We report to Aditheley. Or rather, I'll report to him."

"What will I be doing in the meantime? Keeping watch on Harvington?"

"I don't imagine you fancy a hard ride to Shrewsbury," Stephen said. "It's almost forty miles from here, and I aim to make it in a day. So I thought it best if I go by myself. You can get back to Ludlow on the Cleobury Road from Bewdley. There are plenty of travelers from Bewdley so you won't have to go alone."

Gilbert sighed. "Sparing my poor arse the torture? That is unusually thoughtful of you. I can't say I'm sorry to be getting back home. The food's not been up to standard."

"You could eat at the king's table and find it not up to standard. I'll take some more of that bacon."

Chapter 15

Gilbert was right about one thing: even the stallion's similarities in markings did not prove that it was the one Richard Deme had sold to one of the victims. So Stephen rode first to Stourton to see Deme.

Deme greeted Stephen with shock and astonishment. He flapped his hands and said, "What's happened to you? Why are you dressed like *that*?" That, of course, meant Stephen's archer's clothes. He hadn't taken the time to change.

There was no point in explaining, so he said, "Would you mind coming outside? I want you to look at a horse."

They went out to the courtyard. Deme saw the stallion and exclaimed, "Where did you find him? Ah, you've arrested the killers!"

"No, but I've found out who they are. This is the horse you sold to the lord of Claverley, am I right?"

Deme nodded. "It is. Where are those bastards?"

"Down in Worcestershire."

"Of all places."

"They are a careful bunch. They apparently never raided near home."

Stephen mounted his regular riding horse and picked up the reins for the packhorse and the stallion.

"You'll not … leave him with me?" Deme asked with a hint of avariciousness.

"No. He's evidence. I have to turn him over to the sheriff."

"Of course you do."

Stephen made it in a day to Shrewsbury at the cost of exhausting the horses, but arrived after dark, too late to get into the city. He was lucky to find room on the floor of an inn near the abbey and a place for the horses at that hour. Neither the innkeeper nor the stableman was happy at being roused to attend to him.

He collected the stallion and walked up to the gate over the Severn bridge as the sun peeped over the horizon and the wards pulled open the city gate. Clothed now as a gentryman, he avoided the toll by declaring he was on sheriff's business, entered the town and climbed the long steep hill to the castle; the city occupied a great loop in the River Severn with the castle standing at the narrow neck upon a formidable hill.

Alditheley was still in his chambers when Stephen presented himself in the hall and asked for an audience. It wasn't long, however, before Alditheley came to the stairs, saw Stephen by the central fire and hurried down.

"You have something to report?" Alditheley asked as he settled into a cushioned chair by the fire, which was already burning merrily, putting off enough heat to broil anyone who sat too close.

"I have, sir," Stephen said. He told the sheriff what happened in Harvington and about the stallion.

"What happened to the horse?" Alditheley said.

"I brought it here, to be evidence. Richard Deme says it is the same animal he sold to one of the victims." Stephen paused. "I came straight here as fast as I could. You must make haste to arrest these men. I'm afraid they will attack again after losing that bet with me. They are greedy for money and I've deprived them of a great pile of it."

"You'll have to turn over that pile to me," Alditheley said. "It is doubtless spoils of their robberies."

Stephen handed over a sack he had acquired that morning. It was heavy with pennies and there had been no strong room at the inn to lock it up. A part of him wanted to keep it since he needed money himself so badly. But Alditheley was right; it was the fruit of murder and robbery. Alditheley felt the substantial weight of it and set it by his feet.

The sheriff's fingers drummed on the arm of his chair. His eyes gazed into the distance as thoughts marched at a steady tread through his head. He said, "You will accompany me to make the arrest."

"Me?" Stephens said, surprised.

"You know the ground, since you've been there. And you know the suspects by name and what they look like. So there will be no mistake. I'd hate to hang the wrong man. That could get sticky. You said they were Warwick's people, right? He might take offense to losing an innocent serf."

"Of course, sir. We're going into Worcestershire. Are you sure?"

"What would you have me do? Write to the sheriff there and ask him to do the dirty work?"

"I had supposed that's how it would be done. We don't have any authority in Worcestershire."

"Well, we don't, of course. But have you given any thought to the possibility that there is corruption in play here? None of these attacks occurred in Worcestershire, as far as we know. And it is highly likely that the authorities in that county have some inkling what's going on but have been paid to look the other way. Certainly I would expect the bailiff of the hundred to know something's fishy in this Harvington. Nobody can keep secrets about anything." Alditheley tapped the arm of the chair. "We will swoop in, nab them and be gone before anyone can question it." He cocked an eyebrow. "You're a man who cuts corners. Do you have some objection now?"

"No, sir."

"Good. I have enough men in the garrison so we can be on the road tomorrow. That soon enough for you?"

The garrison numbered forty-five men. Alditheley left five archers behind. It was a dangerous thing to leave the castle so lightly manned, but the sheriff reckoned that he would be back before any enemy found out. His little army thus consisted of twenty-two men-at-arms, three resident knights, and fifteen mounted archers. Together with Alditheley and Stephen that meant forty-two in all. Such a large force riding through Worcestershire would not go unnoticed and was sure to provoke the sheriff's hundred bailiffs to ask questions, so

Kidderminster had to be avoided and the entry into Worcestershire had to be put off until the last leg. Stephen's dash from Stourton to Shrewsbury provided Alditheley with the solution. They rode down to Stourton in a single day, unburdened by baggage and packhorses, thus not having to leave the borders of Shropshire and Staffordshire, and stayed at the castle. It was only eight miles or so from there to Harvington, according to Deme, which was good news. It was even better news that Deme had a man who could serve as a guide to take them down little used tracks to get there.

The eastern sky was lightening when the sheriff's men emerged from the forest. A cart track through pleasant fields stretched before them.

"Is this it?" Alditheley asked Stephen as if he wasn't sure whether to trust the guide.

"Yes," Stephen said. It was the same route he had walked down only a few days ago.

"How much further?"

"A mile and a bit," Stephen said.

"People will be stirring," Alditheley said. "We must pick up the pace."

He broke into a trot and the other men did as well in a disciplined column of twos. It was damp so there was no dust cloud to alert anyone ahead yet of their coming.

When the first houses came into view, Alditheley slowed to a walk. He stretched out his hands and pointed to either side. The three knights, each assigned a contingent, turned off the road one going left and the other two right. They burst into a gallop and charged around the outside of the village. The task of two of the contingents was to prevent anyone fleeing toward the east and the west. The third made for the south of the village, where it would perform the same function as the others.

Alditheley's band continued into the village. At the first houses, men slipped from their horses and entered, emerging with the occupants whom they thrust into the street and went on to the next houses. Those flushed out were herded forward, the captive crowd swelling, a miserable, crying, shouting, protesting puddle of humanity. They could not understand why this was happening in their peaceful part of England, but expected the worst — looting, pillaging and rape. Several men and women tried to bolt into the fields behind the houses but the men in the blocking forces caught them easily. No one was hurt, but several men had bleeding heads from the persuasion they received to get back into the crowd.

It took an hour to thoroughly search every house, shack, barn, haystack, and privy pit.

"Do you see them?" Alditheley asked Stephen.

He had spent the hour scanning the faces of all those who had been collected to point them out, but had not spotted Jackin, Pate, Randel, Roll and Stace, so he had been dreading that question. Had they arrived too late? Had the bandits gone on another foray? Had they managed to hide?

"No, sir, I don't," he said.

"Damn!" Alditheley spat. "You!" he turned to two archers. "Find something to fire the houses."

Stephen was stunned to hear him say this. It was true that if the culprits were hiding out in some secret cranny, flames could drive them into the open. But it ran against what the sheriff had said before: not wanting to overly offend the earl of Warwick. Burning a village would surely inflame the earl. It could be a bluff, but Stephen wasn't certain. Alditheley's rage was genuine, so the threat could be as well.

Stephen, meanwhile, spotted the girl Molle in the crowd. He had a hunch she knew where the five men were hiding, for hiding they had to be if they were still in the village. But singling her out to force information from her could make her a scapegoat once the sheriff's force left. There might be reprisals.

He racked his head for an answer to where they might be. What would he do if he was a robber living in a small village?

144

"Wait!" Stephen shouted. "Not yet!"

He went to the village man closest to him and dragged him away from the mob. Giving the poor fellow a violent shake and raising a fist as if to strike him, Stephen snarled, "Which houses are theirs?"

"Whose houses?" the villager answered in a quavering voice.

"Where Jackin, Pate, Randel, Roll and Stace live. If you don't tell me, you heard the lord. We'll burn the village."

The villager licked his lips and glanced at his neighbors. They were quiet, watching the tableaux, their faces giving no hint what they thought he ought to say. Yet the possibility of losing all they owned was dreadful. It meant starvation and ruin and they all knew it.

At last the villager pointed this way and that. "There, there and there."

"You, you and you, come with me," Stephen snapped to the men-at-arms nearest to him.

He strode to the first house the villager had indicated and went inside.

"We've searched this place already, sir," one of the men-at-arms said.

"Not well enough," Stephen said. "Probe the floors with your swords. Look everywhere, under the beds and chests, even the biers."

"What are we looking for?"

"A hidey-hole."

"I don't understand, sir."

"Probe for something that doesn't feel right, something solid but something that doesn't feel like a stone or a root."

The men set to work and at length they had examined every inch of the house without success, apart from a few stones they dug up and discarded. They went to the next house and repeated the process with the same results. A search of the third house was equally disappointing.

When Stephen and the men-at-arms came out of that last one, he could see Aditheley looking distinctly impatient. Stephen waved but Aditheley did not return the gesture.

At the fourth house they were almost finished when one of the soldiers called out, "Sir! I've got something." The soldier was in the bier from which a cow and a dozen goats had been forced out into the yard, where another soldier had been set to watch them so none escaped. "It feels like wood, sir."

Stephen rushed over to the man. Together they swept old hay clotted with animal dung away from the spot. There they found a set of boards lying in the ground.

"Get those things up," Stephen said.

Two of the men pried up the boards and there they were: Jackin, Pate, Roll and Randel, sitting hunched over in a stone-lined pit.

"Hello, Jackin," Stephen said.

"You!" Jackin said.

"Me," Stephen said.

"A spy!"

"Sadly, yes. Where's Stace?"

"He went off yesterday," Jackin said.

"This will do," Stephen said. There was nothing to be done about the missing Stace. "Get them out and let's go."

The soldiers pulled the four men from the hole one at a time and tied their arms behind their backs.

Now the men were out of the hole, it could be seen that it was filled with loot. Stephen jumped down to get a closer look — piles of leather belt pouches and purses pregnant with money, a stack of swords and daggers, a couple of helmets. He examined some of the pouches and discovered various rings, broaches and other jewelry.

He scrambled out of the pit. "Well, Jack," he said. "I think you've managed to avoid the rack."

Jackin sneered and remained silent. He was a defiant one, not given to surrendering his secrets easily; there was nothing soft about him.

"How's he done that?" asked one of the soldiers.

Stephen gestured to the hole. "No need to force a confession from him. All we need is right there. Take them away. And have others come to collect the loot."

One problem yet remained. Where was the fifth man? He had to be the one who covered up the others.

Stephen went to the back door to order the soldier watching the animals to drive them into the bier. He noticed that in the back garden there was a large oven for baking bread. A very large oven, dome-shaped like a beehive. With a very large mouth at the bottom where the fire was laid but it was evident that no fire had been kindled yet in there. He got down on hands and knees and looked through the mouth.

"Hello, Stace," Stephen said to the man curled up inside. "Hide and seek is over."

"Well done," Alditheley said to Stephen when the captives were brought to him, trussed up, along with all the stolen goods. His eyes wandered over the villagers. "Tell me, did you discover anyone here providing these vipers aid and comfort?"

Now the bandits had been caught, the villagers were cowed and silent and, at this question, they became even more hushed and frightened. What Stephen said next could mean death for anyone he picked out. Of course, he knew that the entire village was in on the robberies and the murders; they had benefited from them as much as any of the culprits. And yet … he thought of the cruelty and indifference of their overlords. One cruelty could justify another but …. Then he thought of Molle, who had warned him of danger probably at great risk to herself. Debts had to be repaid.

"No," he said. "There were not."

Alditheley scowled as if he did not believe this answer. It seemed for a moment that he might dispute it. He was not a stupid man and he undoubtedly surmised that the people of the village both knew about the robberies and murders and sheltered those who had done them. But he had the perpetrators. The proof was clear against them. Taking them and leaving the others was likely not to offend the earl of Warwick as much as if he went after the villagers. The earl's wealth depended on the labor of his villeins, after all. So he said, "If you are satisfied."

He turned his horse. "Bring them! Our work here is done."

Chapter 16

On the way back the sheriff stopped at the horse paddock, where the five prisoners were tied to horses so they would not slow down the retreat by having to walk. Then all the horses were driven out of the paddock and led up the road back to Stourton, the aim being to recover stolen property and to get out of Worcestershire as quickly as possible.

The sheriff spent the remainder of the day at Stourton, basking in the success of his mission and enjoying the admiration of Deme and a few other local lords, who, alerted to the sheriff's presence, came by to pay their respects.

The following day, a knight and a party of men-at-arms took the horses and the loot to Shrewsbury. Proclamations would be sent out for representatives of those killed to assemble on a date certain at Shrewsbury to identify to whom the horses and the stolen items belonged so they could be returned to the victims' heirs. Alditheley expected that not all would show up and that he would be able to keep the remainder for himself; sheriffs' perquisites were broad and ill-defined.

The sheriff, meanwhile, took the prisoners and remaining men to Ludlow, the nearest place in either of his counties that had a decent gaol. After what had happened at Birmingham, he deemed the possibility of gaol-break high and he didn't want these prisoners getting away so they could wreak more havoc on already suffering counties, to say nothing of the damage that might be done to his shining reputation. The fact that the Birmingham gaol break had been carried off by the men already in custody and they seemed to have no other confederates did not alter Alditheley's apprehension. Reputation is a frail flower and must be protected against the chilly gusts of chance.

Stephen took his leave of Alditheley at Galdeford Gate, where the sheriff had his gaol in the pit of one of the towers. Alditheley waved him off with a faint thanks. Stephen took the gesture to mean that his part was done, except for having to testify at a trial in the future. He was glad to put the business behind him and have no other part in it.

Stephen set off toward Bell Lane and home, thinking that he would really like to spend a few days at the manor, where it was peaceful and calm, especially now that the specter of famine had receded; there was still a bit of belt tightening needed but spring was around the bend and with it plenty. He was also eager to see Ida. After he had rested he would turn his mind to the problem of Red John, but right now he did not have to think about it.

He met Wymar descending Bell Lane in the other direction. "My lord," Wymar cried with a broad grin. "You're back — and in one piece!"

"Did you think I'd be in two?" Stephen said.

"Well, Gilbert painted a dreadful picture of your danger!"

Stephen grimaced. "Did he say anything to Ida?"

"Oh, no, he was circumspect. But he told me everything."

"Circumspect? Where did you learn a big word like that?"

"Why, the lady has said I must learn to read if I am to be a knight someday. She is teaching me. Haven't you noticed?"

This revelation took Stephen by surprise. He had not noticed and that fact was irritating. "Let's hope you learn to fight better than you can read."

"Of course, sir. I've not been neglecting my studies in that regard." Wymar grasped Stephen's reins while he dismounted. Then he shouted through the door, "Sir Stephen is back!" before leading the horses across the street to the stable at the Broken Shield.

"Quit making such a racket, you simpleton!" Harry shouted from his shop. "I've got work to do!"

Stephen bumped into Ida at the doorway, for she had rushed there when she heard Wymar call out.

They embraced and then she took one of his arms as they broke apart.

"It's good to see you back without any holes in your head for a change. Come," Ida said, leading him toward his chair by the fire. "I've some news about Red John."

"You've solved it?" Stephen asked, surprised.

"Not exactly. Now, just listen and I'll tell you the story."

At first Ida wasn't sure where or how to begin. It had all been clear in her mind before, but now that she had to deliver her report, everything was a jumble. She understood that some things were important while the rest was mere chaff that required no mention. Yet the chaff flooded through her mind so that she remembered all of it as she struggled to pluck the important bits out for Stephen. There was, of course, how she learned about the man with the crooked arm. And then there was the rest of it ….

"Where do you think you're going?" Ida said to Wymar as she came down from her bedchamber. It was Friday, the third day after the discovery of Red John's body. Wymar was in the hall, rolling up a sleeping blanket and making last minute checks of his kit.

"Back to my lord, of course, lady," Wymar said.

"And where, exactly, is he?" she asked.

"I'm … I'm not certain," Wymar said.

"Did he tell you what he intended to do after you left him?"

"No, lady. He did not say."

"You know he will not still be where you left him."

"I suppose not."

"Then how do you suppose to find him, to catch up?"

"I'll ask people where he went."

"What if no one really knows? He isn't one to confide his thoughts in people." Which often included Ida herself, which was irksome.

"Maybe Gilbert said something," Wymar said sulkily.

"I doubt that as well. Anyway, I require you to remain here," Ida said.

"Yes, lady," Wymar said. His tone was even more sulky. "And what do you wish me to do?"

"Keep the house from burning down and watch that the younger children don't kill themselves, for starters."

"Anything more, lady?" Wymar was appalled at this order but open resistance wasn't in him. His resistance was the covert type, pretend to obey without actual obedience; he had developed foot-dragging to a high art.

Ida couldn't resist a smile at his reaction even though it was unfair to needle the young fellow so. "Yes, see if you can find a traveling party heading to Leintwardine."

"Why, if I can ask," Wymar said, brightening a little at the prospect of escaping the supervision of children.

"I wish to go to the manor and check on things. Joan refuses to allow us to go unescorted." The west road out of Dinham Gate went straight to Leintwardine and passed the lane leading north to Halton Priors so Joan could not object if a traveling party escorted them only as far as the track, where they would be on their own lands and unlikely the target of robbers.

"The roads are dangerous, lady. But I can protect you. No need for a traveling party."

"That may be, but if you don't arrange a traveling party I'll have to fight Joan, and you know how stubborn she can be. Find such a party and I'll relieve you of having to mind the boys."

Wymar made the rounds of all the inns and taverns in the town, and those outside the walls as well, and found such a traveling party leaving Ludlow on the morning of the following Tuesday. Ida, Joan and Wymar rode up Broad Street to the Beast Market that morning to join it. It was cold and breezy beneath an overcast sky. The party consisted of two packhorse trains of a dozen horses each with five armed guards between them. Joan studied the guards, slouched and hungover, with an eye that suggested she did not think much of their fighting prowess. But they had steel helmets, mail coats, swords and shields, so if they couldn't fight off ambushers, they might at least scare them away. If Joan intended to voice any objections, she missed her chance because as soon as the women joined them, the packhorse drivers started their horses out of the Beast Market into High Street. Ida pushed her horse to stay with them. Joan, not much good at horses, kicked her beast a little too hard to follow and it burst into a canter and she took off ahead of all of them, arms and legs flapping as she struggled to stay in the saddle. Wymar had to charge after her and catch her horse. The guards roared with laughter at her embarrassment.

"Go easy on her," said Wymar, eager to display his expertise. "Light pressure with the legs. That's all you need."

"Oh, shut up," Joan said scowling. "And you shut up too, you hooligans!" she said to the guards, who were still shaking with laughter. They paid no heed and one of them flapped his arms like a crow, going, "Awk! Awk!"

Wymar trotted up to the man who was flapping like a crow and, grasping a shoulder as he rode by, pulled him from the saddle.

The guard scrambled to his feet and drew his sword. "You little bastard!" he cried.

Wymar drew his own sword and slid from his horse. "What of it?"

"Enough!" Ida cried. "I'll have the sheriff's men down on you for brawling in the streets."

"Yeah," Wymar said. "You know who that is? Lady Ida Attebrook. Her husband is a deputy sheriff. And that woman's her maid. And I am his squire."

"Saved by a woman, you little runt," the crow man said. But he sheathed his sword and mounted his horse. Drawing a sword on someone in the streets, let alone plain brawling, was a serious offense, after all; never mind the assault on someone close to authority. It was best to let things lie and get away while you could.

"Watch yer back, little man," another of the guards said as he rode by Wymar.

"It's too bad he didn't land a little harder," Joan murmured to Wymar.

"I'll have to work on my dismounting technique," Wymar said.

The ride to Halton Priors was tense after that.

Fortunately, the ride was not long, only about two miles to the track that led away from the road to Halton Priors, which they covered in only half an hour. Nobody made comment when Ida and her party turned away, although there were venomous looks from several of the guards. The worst part of the journey was so quickly done that Ida was a little irritated that she had allowed herself to be persuaded to come with an escort. But the bad mood evaporated when the village came into view. She had not lived there long, and not at all since the burning, but she was developing an affection for it. It was hers and that was what counted.

Francis Bartelot hurried from the village well when Ida, Joan and Wymar rode into the village commons.

"My dear!" Mistress Bartelot clucked. "What are you doing here! You shouldn't be up and about in your condition!"

"I'm fine," Ida protested. "I'm barely two months along."

"Well, you come inside and have some refreshment," Mistress Bartelot said. She took Ida's arm and went with her into the timber house that had been built to replace the stone manor house they had lost last year when the baron's forces raided the village and burned everything in sight.

Mistress Bartelot set Ida in a chair and busied herself with fetching a pitcher of fresh ale and cups for the visitors. Fortified with ale, Ida allowed Mistress Bartelot to spread a blanket over her legs. Mistress Bartelot sat down with a cup herself and launched into a longwinded report on all the recent doings at the manor. It was the most talkative Ida had ever seen her. Ordinarily Mistress Bartelot was a severe woman not given to speech unless it was sharp and critical of some sin or misdeed. But manor life had worked a change. She had been born on a manor herself, but as the last of many daughters her family lacked the resources to make her a good marriage with another member of the gentry and she had been married off to a townsman instead. As an elderly widow with her children moved away, she had been a shut-away in her house, the very one that the Attebrooks now occupied. Now that she had fresh air to breathe and a manor to run her sallow cheeks were rosy and her eyes bright.

"Would it be too much trouble if I took a look at the accounts?" Ida said when Mistress Bartelot paused for breath.

"Of course not, my dear. I shall take you there."

There was the little chapel standing behind the walls that had failed to defend the stone house during the raid. The manor's records were kept there in a locked chest. There was no resident cleric to act as secretary so Mistress Bartelot and the other steward, Randulfus, did that work themselves.

Ida and Mistress Bartelot crossed the yard arm-in-arm — Mistress Bartelot seemed to have adopted Ida as a daughter, not that the younger woman minded. The yard itself had not changed any, although the grass was longer than it should be. Ida made a mental note to have some sheep turned loose here to get it under control. It was the ruin of the house that was the most depressing. Two walls had collapsed so that the interior was visible, but at least the charred timbers of its superstructure had been removed. Only weeds grew there now in a hollow shell.

The chapel was small and dim, but Mistress Bartelot unlocked the document chest and set about opening the unusually large windows so that there was plenty of light.

"I must get back," Mistress Bartelot said. "You never know what mischief people will get up to when you're not looking."

"Thank you, Mistress," Ida said, taking a seat at the slanted writing table. A rather chilly breeze came through those windows and she pulled her cloak about her. If and when they had the money, she would install glazes in the windows; it was expensive but made buildings more comfortable.

She spent the next two hours looking over the accounts. It was slow and dreadful work, examining each entry and tallying them up to root out any errors in addition, checking the payments against what the accounts said was left in their little treasury. She would have to count that too, but the money box was back in the timber manor house.

She was just wrapping up when a servant girl came to the door and announced that dinner would be served in a quarter hour.

Dinner conversation revolved around how the sowing of the spring wheat was going, repairs to the barn room which had been damaged in a recent storm, whether something needed to be done to ensure adequate fertilizer for the fields, and how everyone was doing with their back gardens, which were an important source of food.

As dinner broke up and everyone went back to work, Randulfus took Ida to his bedchamber, where the money box was chained to a post since they had no strong room. He shut the door as he went out. Counting money was another tedious chore and there was always the problem of forgetting the count and having to start over. Fortunately, they had a small board with pebbles that you put down to mark when you reached a shilling and then a pound, which helped.

Well into the task after an hour, Ida heard voices raised in the yard. She ignored them but they got louder and continuous. A voice screamed and she dashed to the window to see what was the fuss, with a mind to demand people quiet down and get back to work, but the spectacle that met her eyes caused the words to stick in her throat.

Wymar and another village boy his age were fighting with staves while standing on a board that had been laid over the village pig pen. Some pigs were kept in large runs, but this was a small one. The board stretched clear across it, ten feet at least. While the villagers who had gathered around the pen were enjoying the fun, the pigs were indignant, squealing and wheeling about beneath the two young men. The scream had come from one of the pigs, not a woman in distress.

This could not be tolerated. Fighting with staves was a dangerous business by itself. Staves might look like harmless pieces of wood, but a blow from one could knock a man's brains out. Ida raced downstairs to put a stop to it.

Randulfus was nowhere to be seen when Ida reached the yard. Mistress Bartelot was at the back of the crowd, shouting for order, but no one was paying her any attention. Ida shouted too, but her small voice was lost in the happy clamor.

She pushed her way to the front of the crowd. Her intention was to get everyone's attention when they could see her. But as she reached the fence, Wymar knocked his opponent's staff aside and, lunging forward, thrust him on the shoulder. The blow knocked the fellow off the board. He landed on his back in the mud, with pigs cavorting about him. Wymar, however, did not remain on the board either — the vigor of his lunge unbalanced him and he fell off the other side. Pigs sniffed at his head; he was lucky none of them tried taking a bite out of him — pigs were not discriminating in their tastes and were known to feed on people as readily as anything else.

Both young men promptly clambered to their feet to avoid the pigs and leaped over the fence, dripping with muck, the stench of pig clinging to them so that everyone nearby backed away as fast as they could. There is nothing more revolting than the stench of pig. No matter how hard you tried, you never really got used to it.

The shouting died away.

"What is the meaning of this?" Ida raged. People avoided her eye and those at the back of the crowd started slipping away. "Wymar? Explain yourself."

Wymar looked abashed. "Law here, he said, he …"

"He said what?" Ida demanded.

"He said that I was false, a big pretender, too big for my stockings. That I ought not to be … what I am. That I ought to give it up and go back where I belong." Before being recruited as Stephen's squire, Wymar had been a minor groom here, one of the lesser people of no account in anyone's eyes;

no one really understood why Stephen preferred him when in the village's estimation there were other more worthy candidates.

"I see," Ida said. "It is not Law's place to question the duty chosen for you. But that does not excuse this. I will have both of you up before the next manor court for disturbing the peace. You reek of pig. Mistress Bartelot, see that Wymar is cleaned up. I'll not have him in the house like that."

Mistress Bartelot took this assignment to heart. She marched Wymar to the village well, where he was made to strip off his sodden, pig-soiled clothes down to his braises, then buckets of water were drawn from the well and poured over him while he danced about and shivered. Law got the same treatment from his mother and two other women, who shivered with suppressed laughter when a bucket released its contents. Rough lye soap was found and added to the process, increasing the discomfort, for it was as abrasive as a cake of sand and Mistress Bartelot did not spare in her efforts to soap away the mire.

Ida returned to work and hurried through the rest of the accounting. She had not planned to stay overnight and she began to worry about letting Wymar into the townhouse in his present condition. Was a bucket bath on the common enough to render him approachable? She had her doubts.

At length, Ida finished tallying up the pennies, relieved that the count was consistent with what she found in the records.

Mistress Bartelot, meanwhile, had found a set of clothes for Wymar and allowed him into the hall, although he was confined to a bench against a wall at some distance from everyone else. His hair hung in clotted strings about his miserable face and gave the appearance of still harboring muck from the pig pen. Ida sniffed his head and her suspicions were confirmed.

"Get our horses ready," she told Wymar. "We're going back."

"Yes, lady," Wymar said and fled from of the hall.

He stuck his head back in shortly to announce that all was ready for their departure. Mistress Bartelot tossed him a sack containing his soiled clothes.

"Waste of a good sack," she sniffed. "You might as well burn it when you're done." No one would, of course. A good sack was as valuable as a decent shirt and it would be washed with the rest.

Out in the yard, Joan looked off to the south toward the road back to Ludlow. She seemed anxious although she tried not to show it. But Ida knew her too well, and it suddenly occurred to her that, tough as she was, Joan was even more nervous about being on the road and the possibility of kidnapping as Ida was herself. The last time had been a terrifying experience and both of them still had terrible dreams about it.

"Wymar," Ida said. "You know the manor. Is there a way to get back to the Dinham Bridge without taking the road?"

Wymar bobbed his head. "Yes, lady. The fields are full of tracks that wend that way. It will take longer but it can be done."

"Then show us the way."

It turned out to be a more pleasant ride than along the road. The fields to the north bordering the manor's forest were lying fallow this year and were covered in bright grass. Many of the village cattle and sheep grazed here. Other fields were sprouting with the winter wheat, the stalks rising green and tall, defiant of bad weather. Yet others were being plowed and sown by parties of men for barley and spring wheat. The smell of freshly turned earth was in the air. It was all tidy and good.

These byways led them at last to the road where it turned round the base of Whitcliffe, steep and wooded, and the castle crept into view upon its hill. From there it was but a short dash to the bridge.

Ida made up her mind what had to be done about Wymar only when they rode down Bell Lane and stopped before the Broken Shield Inn.

"Put up the horses," she said to Wymar. "We'll wait for you here."

"Here?" Wymar asked, puzzled. "In the street?"

"You heard me."

Wymar nodded, glum-faced, no doubt thinking that Ida had devised some cunning punishment for him from the stern way she had addressed him.

Joan was as mystified as Wymar about what Ida intended but she did not ask questions. She talked with Harry through the window to see how his work was going. Ida counted the farthings in her purse and decided she had just enough.

"Harry, is it too early for you to knock off?" Ida asked.

"There's still a couple of hours of daylight left, but I suppose so, if the reason's good," Harry said.

Meanwhile, Wymar emerged from the stable gateway.

"Wymar, help Harry with his cart," Ida said. "Don't bother with the pony. You pull it instead."

So that was it, eh? Wymar's face said. I'm to be humiliated before the entire town. Me, a noble squire, forced to play the part of a cart horse.

There was a moment when it seemed that Wymar might rebel, but he went inside the house as he was told.

Harry could be heard to exclaim, "God's bunions, man! What happened to you?"

"He fell in a pigsty!" Joan called through the doorway before Wymar could make up some face-saving story.

"I thought I smelled pig. Even Gilbert couldn't manage something like that," Harry's said.

It wasn't long before Wymar appeared in the alley beside the house in the traces of Harry's pony cart. Harry sat in his usual place with his whip swishing back and forth.

"Where are we going?" Harry asked.

"The Kettle," Ida said.

"Ah! Sensible! Make haste, good steed," Harry said to Wymar.

"If you call me that one more time, you can walk," Wymar gritted.

"Wymar, Stephen has pulled Harry's cart a time or two," Ida said. "It won't hurt you to do it."

The Kettle, or as it was formally known the Wobbley Kettle, was the town's only bath house. It stood by one of the town mills at the foot of Ludford Bridge under the sign of a red kettle tipped on its side spilling blue water. It was a popular gathering spot. The fact there were whores working the place didn't make it so disreputable that ladies couldn't go there, as it had two halls, one for men and a second for women who did not wish to be exposed to the flesh trade.

Ida led them through the door into the smaller women's hall and ordered tubs for everyone. She paid for them all, especially Wymar, to ensure that he had a bath and not something else (assuming that any woman, even one whose tastes were blunted by avarice, would have him). It was all rather expensive since Harry and Joan had a tub themselves, as did Ida. While it was not uncommon for both sexes to share a tub even if unrelated, she had never been comfortable with that, unless Stephen was her companion. Wymar had to share a tub but Ida could not afford sympathy for those who had to put up with him.

Bathing was a luxurious experience. The water was often tepid rather than hot at the end of the day and frequently a scum of dirt from prior bathers floated on the surface, but even so it was a pleasure that relaxed the body and calmed the mind. Ida lulled in the warmth, the back of her head against the top of the tub, feeling that she could fall asleep. A woman attendant entered and dipped her finger into the water.

"Iveta!" the attendant shouted. "More water in number three!"

Ida jerked out of her reverie as if she had been slapped on the face. She looked around as a thin girl in shabby clothes came through the opening in the curtains, lugging two full buckets hanging from a bar resting on her shoulder.

"Careful there, you idiot!" the attendant said. "Don't spill any!" Hot water was precious; it took a lot of wood to heat it.

"Sorry," the girl muttered. She set the buckets down.

Ida was so surprised at this that she stood up, goosepimples immediately erupting all over her body.

Both the girl and the attendant looked at Ida, standing there naked, with astonishment.

"Is there a problem, m'lady?" the attendant asked.

"No," Ida said, shivering in the cold air. "I need to speak with this girl. Could you hand me a towel?"

The attendant handed Ida a towel which she wrapped around her shoulders and stepped out of the tub. The towel helped with the chill but not much.

"You're Iveta," Ida said.

"That's what people call me."

The attendant slapped Iveta on the back of the head. "Mind your manners. You're talking to Lady Ida Attebrook."

"M'lady," Iveta muttered.

"Has she done something wrong?" the attendant asked.

"No," Ida said. "But I have some questions for her. Could you give us a moment?"

The attendant nodded and left. But Ida could feel her lingering beyond the curtain to overhear what was said next. Ida waited a heartbeat then stuck her head through the gap in the curtains. As she suspected, the attendant was there.

"I will speak to the girl out of your hearing, if you please," Ida said as coldly as she could manage. "As I said, it has nothing to do with the service here."

"As you wish, m'lady," the attendant said grudgingly. She withdrew toward the hall.

Ida pulled the curtain closed.

"You've just recently come to town, have you not?" Ida asked Iveta.

"I'm not going back! No matter what!" Iveta said hotly.

"Back where?" Ida said involuntarily, unaware that the conversation had veered from the line she intended to take.

"The manor."

"What manor?"

"Richard's Castle," Iveta said.

"You've run away."

"What if I have?" Iveta said defiantly. "Go ahead. You can tell the lord. I'll be gone by tomorrow. He won't catch me."

"I have no intention of telling your lord anything about you," Ida said as understanding dawned. The girl was a runaway serf. She feared being sent back. Runaways were often punished harshly. "What I want is information — information that I believe only you possess."

Iveta regarded Ida with measuring eyes as calculating as any adults and more than a little anxiety. "This is about that tavern keeper."

"Yes, Red John. What have you to say about him?"

"You won't tell on me?"

"No. I promise."

Iveta crossed her arms. Her eyes focused into the distance. She said, "I'd just got to town that very day. Snuck in with a pack train through Broad Gate. I tried a little begging, but didn't get anything. Then night came and I had to find a place out of the cold. The tavern, it's down some steps. I thought I might get out of the wind there. I was hunkered down when three fellows came down the steps."

"When was this?"

"I don't know. About an hour or so after the bells rang."

That is, about an hour after curfew.

"What happened?" Ida asked.

"They weren't happy to find me there. One of them dragged me up to the street. They had to, to get around me. The steps are narrow. Another said, 'Get rid of her.' The one who had hold of me reached for his dagger, but I kicked him in the privates and managed to break free and run."

"He didn't chase you?"

"No, he wasn't in no shape for that. Anyway, no man can catch me even if he tried."

"Do you remember anything about this man? Or any of them? Anything that stands out in your mind?"

"I didn't see them well. It was dark down those stairs. In moon shadow, you know. But the one who hauled me up had a funny arm."

"What do you mean by a funny arm?"

"It was bent, like."

"How so?"

"Here." Iveta touched a spot a few inches above her left wrist. "It was bent, like a twig."

"It was the left arm?"

"Yes."

"And you didn't get a good look at his face?"

Iveta shook her head. "I wasn't paying too much attention to that at the time."

Ida finished the story of all she had done. After speaking to Iveta, she'd felt she had discovered the key to everything and had floated on a gauzy sense of triumph for at least a day afterward. But now that she had spoken of it in cold hard words, it seemed a piece of nothing.

Stephen listened to her report, face grave. "You have been busy. It's something, at least."

"I hope so, but now I don't know," Ida said.

"It proves, at least, that we're looking for a man with a crooked arm," Stephen said thoughtfully. "You've also shown that the killers knew enough to stay at the Trumpet. They knew Jacky and Abby wouldn't ask questions like they might get at the Broken Shield or the Jolly Turtle. It means they are familiar with the town. So I bet that this crooked-armed fellow probably came from somewhere around here. It shouldn't be impossible to find a man with such a deformity. Did you ask Harry if he knew anyone like that?"

"She did," Harry said. "And no, I don't."

Chapter 17

Stephen went up to the gaol the next morning. A thought had occurred to him during the night which had greatly disturbed his ability to sleep. It needed urgent attention, a dreadful burr that continued to annoy even now when nighttime obsessions revealed themselves to be nothings. If anything, his unease had grown.

"Ah, come to see the sheriff?" the gaoler said, rising from his stool in the ground floor of one of Galdeford Gate's towers. "I'm afraid you've just missed him. He's gone out."

"No," Stephen said. "I have other business."

He knelt and grasped the handle to the trapdoor that opened above the prison pit beneath their feet.

"Sir!" the gaol exclaimed. "What!"

"I need to talk to one of the prisoners." Stephen pulled up the heavy door and let it fall open with a great thunk.

"Sir! I've strict orders!" the gaoler protested as Stephen kicked the rope ladder used to get into and out of the pit through the aperture. "They're a desperate lot. They've done gaol breaks before."

"Are you accusing me of helping them escape?"

"No, sir. It's just, I've my orders, sir. The sheriff don't want to take no chances."

"This is on my authority, then," Stephen said. Little as that authority might mean.

"Jackin! Jackin Brekebac!" he called into the dark hole, where nothing could be seen. "Out now!"

There was some delay and then the rope ladder began to jerk as someone began the long climb. At length, Jackin's head and shoulders emerged from the gloom. Stephen drew his dagger, grasped Jackin by his coat and hauled him the rest of the way with a violent jerk. He was a heavy, broad-shouldered man and the strain made Stephen, more lean and quick, grunt with the effort. Yet Jackin popped out of the hole like a rabbit plucked from his den. He landed on his stomach.

Stephen pressed his knee to Jackin's back and the point of his dagger to Jackin's neck. "Don't move if you don't want a taste of steel."

"All right, all right," Jackin said, his mouth to the floor.

Stephen glanced back to ensure that no one else was on the ladder. He motioned to the gaoler to shut the trap door.

"Bind his hands," Stephen ordered.

Stephen remained with his dagger to Jackin's neck while the gaoler tied his wrists. Then he flipped Jackin onto his back. Jackin struggled to sit up.

"Having fun down there?" Stephen asked.

"I could use a drink," Jackin said.

"You'll be lucky to get water," Stephen said. He waved to the gaoler to bring the water bucket forward. He held it so Jackin could drink, getting a good part of the bucket on his chest.

When Jackin had his drink, Stephen told the gaoler, "Lower what's left for the others."

"What do you want?" Jackin said as the gaoler pulled open the trap door and, after raising the rope ladder as a precaution against ambush, lowered the bucket.

"You know we've enough to hang you. It won't take five minutes for the jury to return its verdict. So you lose nothing by helping me."

Jackin shrugged. "I said, what do you want? Not to give me presents, I'm sure."

"I want information," Stephen said.

"I don't know nothing," Jackin said.

"How are they feeding you?" Stephen asked, knowing that the prisoners were lucky to get oat porridge with perhaps a sweetening of mouse dung no more than once a day.

"I wouldn't call that slop food," Jackin said.

"If you answer my questions truthfully, I'll have a meal sent to you."

Jackin's face glittered with calculation. "What about the others?"

"Them, too."

"Is this a sly way of getting a confession?"

"This isn't about what you've done. It's about what you haven't done."

"I don't follow."

"On the last day of February a certain William Griffin of Fox Hall Manor was murdered and robbed about two miles outside of Bewdley in the Wyre Forest on his way home, along with his groom. Was that your work?"

"Outside Bewdley you say? In the Wyre Forest? Just a few weeks ago?" He stared into Stephen's eyes with an unwavering gaze. There was a long silence. Then he said, "We had nothing to do with that."

"It's too close to home, isn't it," Stephen said, his eyes locked on Jackin's which had not wavered yet. He had the suspicion that Jackin could lie convincingly and yet he had the feeling that in this Jackin was telling the truth. Feelings, however, were not evidence and they often led you astray.

"My mother always said never shit in your own house," Jackin said.

"Wise woman," Stephen said. "There's one other thing. When we went through the village there was no sign of a crossbow."

"Why's that interest you?"

"Do any of you use a crossbow?"

"We're stout English country lads. Crossbows are for the gentry, or foreigners. We're all longbow men," Jackin said with some pride, as well he should have done, since he had stood in battle and done his best, a good man whom circumstances, temptation and spite had turned bad.

"Is there more?" Jackin asked to fill an uncomfortable silence that had settled in.

"No. It's back to your hole, I'm afraid."

"And that meal?"

"I'll have it sent up this afternoon."

167

"Feelings are most unreliable things," Gilbert said that evening in the hall of the Broken Shield after Stephen had recounted his conversation with Jackin. "Tricky, that's what they are."

"I knew you'd say that," Stephen said.

"Then why don't you take my advice and not rely on them?"

"Well, there are other things besides. The fact they don't use crossbows."

"So he says. Another feeling."

"We didn't find any at Harvington in any of their houses or anywhere else."

"The absence of evidence of a thing doesn't prove it's not there."

"What about the fact that all the attacks that can with confidence be attributed to Jackin all occurred on the east side of the Severn?"

"You forget, there were attacks on the road connecting Bridgnorth and Cleobury that were similar."

Gilbert was right about that. Both those places lay to the west of the Severn.

"The only way to be really sure is the thumbscrew or hot iron," Gilbert said.

"Are you serious?"

"No, but I wondered if in your desperation you would stoop to that."

"I think I'll stick with feelings."

"Life is full of gambles, isn't it?"

"That's funny coming from you. One of the men most averse to gambling I've ever met." Stephen poured himself another cup of small ale. "But what if Jackin's telling the truth? It means that there might be another gang of killers out there — the same ones, maybe, who attacked us. One of them had a crossbow."

"This is the first time I've heard that. Why didn't you say something about it before?"

"I don't know. Slipped my mind, I guess."

"The presence of that crossbow would support a conclusion that our attackers were the same as the ones who killed Griffin. But if they weren't the same men you arrested in Worcestershire, it's odd that this supposed other gang slashed Griffin's face," Gilbert said.

"What if this other gang is copying the Harvington gang's methods — to throw off suspicion?"

"I suppose that could be. But that grants robber gangs more intelligence that I would expect from them."

"But this gang isn't a bunch of angry villeins. From the evidence at least one of them was a man-at-arms —"

"Could have been a man-at-arms," interjected Gilbert.

"He could be led by a local lord, someone with cunning. A war leader accustomed to stratagems and deceptions. It wouldn't be the first time a lord stooped to robbery."

"Speculation," Gilbert said. "Aren't you underestimating the ability of simple villeins? They aren't stupid, you know. The gentry don't have monopoly on cleverness."

"Have you got anything to offer other than criticism?" Stephen said, exasperated that Gilbert had suddenly shifted positions. "You haven't been too helpful."

"My task in life is to keep you firmly tethered to the earth. Isn't that helpful enough?" Gilbert sighed. "But no. Frankly I do not. I shall have to yield to your feelings as well and see where they lead."

"Except for the man with the crooked arm," Stephen said rather bleakly. "We can be certain about that."

"But until such a man is found there's nothing we can do for Red John."

There was still at least half an hour of daylight left when Stephen entered Bell Lane. His tired feet — his bad foot protested all the work it had been forced to do during the day even though that hadn't amounted to much — voted for retreat into the townhouse and settling by the fire, with a nice hot bucket for the bad one to make amends for the abuse it had suffered. But thoughts of the man with the crooked arm lingered in his mind. Ida had uncovered something important there and had taken the inquiry a long way toward its solution. If only there was a way to find that man.

With such thoughts looming large, Stephen turned down Bell Lane toward Broad Street.

It was but half a mile from the Broken Shield to the house of Will Thumper on Lower Galdeford Road just beyond the Augustinian priory, and only took about ten minutes or so of swift striding to get there, the bad foot objecting to every step on the way.

Calling Will Thumper's manse a house was being charitable. It consisted of three parts, a central one with two wings, one on each end that had been added later so the whole had a lopsided U shape. The central part, which held the hall and assorted chambers, had the look of an old barn that had reached the end of its useful life, sagging with fatigue and hardly able to hold up its thatched roof. The yard was littered with old bits of lumber, shattered handcarts, and piles of compost.

As often happened the Thumper lookouts — they kept a good watch on every coming and going, for the Thumpers' occupation was well outside the law — alerted those within the house of Stephen's approach, and Will Thumper himself opened the door as Stephen crossed the yard.

"What's the trouble now?" Will asked suspiciously. He was a short muscular fellow in his early forties with gray-streaked black hair. A blunt, pugnacious nose and wary eyes dominated his face.

"Trouble?" Stephen said.

"There's always trouble when you show up. Anyway, now that you're a deputy sheriff, it's probably not a good idea to have anything to do with you."

"I know your secrets, Will. You know I know about your little storeroom over there, filled to the eaves with property that doesn't belong to you. Yet I've said nothing."

"Uh-huh."

"Look, I need your help again."

Will crossed his muscular thick arms. "No more running around asking questions. That was so damned tedious. I could hardly keep the boys at it." A few months ago, Stephen had paid the Thumpers, a clan so numerous that nobody had any idea how many there were, to find out some information that was important to a murder he was trying to solve. This involved questioning every household in Ludlow and its surroundings.

"This will be a bit different. I just need your boys to keep a lookout for someone and send back word if they spot him."

"All right, I suppose. What's his name?"

"I don't have a name for him. That's the problem. But I do know one thing about him. He has a crooked left forearm. It's bent a few inches above the wrist, from a fall or something. I think he lives somewhere nearby."

"What's this about? Red John?"

Stephen nodded.

"I always liked him," Will said. "A decent fellow."

"I think the man with the crooked arm is one of those who killed him."

"I wouldn't mind catching them. But what's in it for us if we help out?" The Thumpers never did anything for free. Even putting an ear to the ground, so to speak, had its cost.

"There's a reward offered by his cousin for information leading to the arrest of those responsible."

"How much?"

"Ten pounds."

Will whistled. "Whoa! I could turn honest for that amount of money. I'll put the word out."

Chapter 18

Bewdley was a small town that huddled at the foot of a steep hill on the banks of the River Severn. It had two reasons for being: the first was the presence of a ferry across the river and the second was as a port, where goods were brought up from Gloucester and Bristol to be carried inland by packtrain, wagon and cart in exchange for goods brought here for carriage south, such as much of the region's wool clip. Its houses gathered mainly along its main street, Lode Street, which ran down to the river from a stone church occupying the junction where three roads branching out from the village climbed away to their distant destinations, north, west and south.

Stephen and Gilbert rode down the steep hill and passed the church, glad to have reached the place at last after a slow day's ride. Gilbert had a blister on his bum from his ride back to Ludlow; it had not healed and caused him considerable discomfort so that he had elected to walk much of the way. It was nearing sundown and the church cast a long shadow down Lode Street. There were five inns about the church. Gilbert rejected the first one because it had a bad smell but found the next one acceptable, especially because they were able to secure a chamber that they didn't have to share with anyone else and thus avoided being subjected to foreign burps, farts, coughs, sneezes, assorted rustlings and tossings and turnings, and the bumping about that came when people staggered up to find the chamber pot during the night. There was nothing less conducive to a good night's rest than being stepped on or crawled over by a late-night wanderer.

Gilbert threw himself face down on the chamber's bed and moaned, "My poor bum!" a refrain that he had uttered for most of the journey. "I hate horses! And they don't love me!"

Although Stephen had strived to be sympathetic, he was tired of hearing Gilbert's complaints after a long day of having to listen to them. But he still held back the rebuke ("Then you should have stayed home!") that he yearned to deliver. Instead he said, "I saw an apothecary up the street. I'll see if they have a salve for what ails you."

"My savior!" Gilbert said.

"It would pain me to watch you having to fill your stomach while standing up," Stephen said.

"Oh, my. I hadn't thought of that. What would people say?"

"If you had a reputation it would surely be ruined," Stephen said.

"Well, hurry back. I'm hungry. Isn't it time for supper?"

"You think it's always time for supper," Stephen said as he retreated from the room.

The apothecary was only a few doors from the inn. The apothecary, a long-fingered man, said he had just the thing when Stephen inquired about salves for saddle sores and riding blisters. He plunked a clay bottle on the counter and named his price, which was ungodly expensive considering how little there had to be in that bottle.

"I hope Gilbert appreciates this," Stephen said to himself as he counted out the required number of farthings. As he handed over the money, he asked, "Oh, by the way, can you tell me where I can find the Paddoc house?"

The apothecary looked him up and down with newly appraising eyes. "Looking for Ingrede, are you?" He scoffed. "Another suitor!" He called over his shoulder to someone out of view. "Another suitor for Ingrede!"

"Of course, there is," a feminine voice replied.

"Your sort hasn't wasted any time coming out of the woodwork since Griffin died," the apothecary said.

"And just when we thought we were rid of her!" the feminine voice called from its concealment.

"She's trouble?" Stephen said.

"We've already had one man killed because of her. In the street not more than fifty feet from where we stand," the apothecary said. "A quarrel between suitors. One tried to run the other off with threats and it went to steel from there."

"I'm not a suitor," Stephen said.

"A strapping, handsome fellow like you? Of course, you're not," the apothecary said without the slightest sign he believed the claim. "But I can't have you wandering aimlessly about calling for Ingrede. Her house is on the quay. Go to the foot of Lode Street, turn left, third house."

"I'm obliged," Stephen said, taking the bottle and his leave.

"You're wasting your time," the apothecary said to his back.

Stephen turned aside at the inn to leave the bottle with Gilbert, who was still face down on the bed. Stephen set the bottle by him and said, "You'll have to put it on yourself. I'm not touching you."

"But I'm not sure I can reach the place in my present condition," Gilbert moaned.

"You'll have to do your best. I'm going to find Ingrede."

"Wait! I'm going too. I want to see this fabled beauty."

Gilbert staggered from the bed with additional groans and they set off for the quay.

Lode Street ended at the river in what appeared to be a natural cut through the bank; this was where the ferry operated. At one time, the bank now occupied by the quay must have been steep and lined with trees as the banks beyond the limits of the village. But at some point in the distant past, the villagers had put in a wooden wall on the bank's face, cut with numerous steps to reach the boats that tied up there one against the other so that you could walk the length of the town quay upon them at the busiest times.

The third house down was, like its neighbors, timber and wattle, its limewash a light pink that pleased the eye and contrasted sharply with the deep green door. There was no sign to identify its occupant or the business that the shop in the front conducted; a gate by the side of the house indicated there was a courtyard beside and beyond the house and probably a warehouse.

As they drew up, a tall man, obviously a high-born, came out of the house. Black-haired and hawk faced, he was dressed to impress in a gold-embroidered cap, a striped tunic decorated with sparkling silver buttons and hanging sleeves, and knee-high boots with well-pointed toes dyed a brilliant red. His fierce eyes locked on Stephen's first with curiosity and then, as they passed and Stephen halted at the door, turned hostile. His arrogant mouth twisted down in immediate dislike. Leaving behind a disdainful look he turned away and stalked up the quay to Lode Street, where he met two men who had to be retainers and turned the corner.

Stephen looked into the open shop window. There was a thick-set middle-aged man seated at a table examining documents, twirling a feather pen in blunt ink-stained fingers. Curiously, an unsheathed sword leaned against the table at his elbow as if he expected trouble at any moment. Scribe he appeared to be, but even sitting down he gave the impression of a man who knew how to take care of himself.

"Is this the Paddoc house?" Stephen asked.

The pen wielder looked up from his documents. "It is. Have you business here?"

"I'm looking for Ingrede Paddoc. Is she home?"

The pen wielder set down his pen. "Let me guess. You've come to pay your respects."

"No, I haven't. My sympathies, perhaps on the death of her fiancé. But that's it."

The scribe seemed no more convinced than the apothecary. "She's busy."

"How do you know?"

The scribe shrugged. "A wild guess."

"Why don't we do this. My name is Stephen Attebrook. I'm a deputy sheriff for Shropshire and Staffordshire. I am tasked with investigating the death of William Griffin. I would like to speak to her in that capacity."

"This is Worcestershire. You've no authority here."

"I haven't the authority to arrest anyone, but there is nothing that says I can't ask questions. That's what you do in a murder inquiry, by the way. You ask questions until you arrive at the truth."

"The mistress doesn't know anything about Lord Griffin's death."

"Perhaps not directly. But perhaps something she knows might be helpful. Now run off and tell her I'm waiting."

The scribe looked as though he might defy this request. But then he hauled himself to his feet and lumbered to the hall behind the shop.

Presently the front door opened. A vision of young womanhood stood there, only partially revealed but enough to see she was stunning. She was tall, almost as tall as Stephen, and supple and shapely. A thick auburn braid spilled out of the modest scarf about her head and hung over her right shoulder as far as her waist. Gray intelligent and measuring eyes regarded him levelly. Her carriage was calm and confident, giving the impression that she was older than her actual age. The apothecary said men had died dueling over her and Stephen could see why.

"You've come to ask about William?" Ingrede said. "About why he died and who killed him?"

"That is my task, our task," Stephen said.

"What more possibly needs to be done? News has come to us that the villains responsible for all those terrible robberies and murders have been caught. Surely they were the ones who killed William."

"I don't think so," Stephen said. "Those men are rustics, serfs, with a deep resentment of the better classes for wrongs done to them, not that that excuses what they've done. But we are certain that one of those who killed William Griffin was a man-at-arms and not any of the men in custody are such men. Likely in the employ of some lord, little or big, we don't know yet."

"Could it be another gang, then, one not connected with them?" Ingrede asked.

"We are considering that possibility."

She held the door fully open. "Come in."

She led them into the hall where they found seats by the hearth fire. She sat across from Stephen and Gilbert. The scribe stood behind her, his attitude protective.

"Are you her father?" Stephen asked the scribe.

"No, I am Bernard, an employee."

"Father is on the river," Ingrede said. She smiled fondly. "Bernard watches over me in his absence to see that I don't get into trouble."

"More to keep the trouble away from you, although I haven't been very successful at it," Bernard said.

"You blame yourself too much," Ingrede said.

"I am sorry for your loss," Stephen said awkwardly by way of turning the conversation to the reason why he was here.

"William was a good man," she said. "He was kind, and many mistook that for weakness. But he was strong when it counted."

"I'm told you've been much pursued," Stephen said.

"That is an understatement," Bernard snorted.

"I just heard a tale that there was a duel in the street over you," Stephen said. "That a man died of it."

"People blame me for it," Ingrede. "But how can I control what men do?"

"Could there have been other men who took the news of your betrothal to William Griffin in the same way?"

"I'm not sure."

"One of those enamored of you is Baron Plumton, Richard Plumton," Stephen said.

"He was one of those involved in the duel," Ingrede said. "He is an important man in Worcestershire, a cousin to our sheriff, William de Beauchamp, which is why he is free while awaiting his pardon and not in gaol. He is a vain man, avaricious, given to bouts of violent temper. He does not like being denied what he wants." A delicate hand rose to her mouth. "I have wondered …"

"That he might be the one instead of the gang of villeins?"

"I confess the thought occurred to me. He ill-used his first wife. It's said that he beat her so severely that she died. Although no accusation has ever formally been made." Her eyes rose to his. "But then we heard how William was mutilated, like others in Shropshire and Staffordshire. I don't think murder is beyond Richard but I cannot imagine him violating a dead man so."

"Tell me, does Plumton have a man with a scar on his lip here?" Stephen indicated the spot on the left side of his mouth, "And a crooked, rather flat nose? He would be a hard looking man, soldierly."

Ingrede searched her memory in silence for some time. "I can't say that he does. At least I've never seen such a man. But Richard has many men at his disposal."

"Has Plumton made overtures to you since Griffin's death?" Stephen asked.

Ingrede nodded. "Even now, today. In fact, he was just leaving as you arrived. The game begins again," she said bitterly. "None of my gentleman suitors offers marriage. Oh no, I'm too common for that, a riverman's daughter without the manners, refinement or lands of a proper wife. They want a bed pony, a mistress. They promise houses, estates, allotments of money, the world if only I throw myself on my back for them. All except William. He wanted a wife."

"So that was Plumton?" If Plumton were here it would be a simple matter to look over his entourage for the flat-nose man. "Do you happen to know where he's staying?"

"His chief manor of Hartley Green lies about five miles from here on the road to Worcester. He prefers to spend his nights there. Bewdley is too small and rough for his taste."

Night had fallen at last on a weary town but it was still too early for most travelers to go to bed or the inns and taverns to quit serving drink, as there was no curfew in the town, nor any night watch. The town wasn't rich enough for a bailiff to enforce a curfew — there were only two and their main job was to maintain order, that is, prevent fights — nor was there enough money for a night watch. The lack of a curfew meant the taverns and halls of the inns stayed open late to serve their chief customers, the rivermen, who would drink and gamble all night if they could. So here and there down Lode Street lights shown around windows shuttered against the wind and evening's chill, proof that the businesses were still dishing out merriment to those who could afford it and a few who could not.

The hall of their inn was no exception. It was crowded and noisy. The harried servants bustled about bearing fresh pitchers and carrying away empty ones while games of chance flourished upon many of the tables and in the corners. The fire was high and hot and smoky. One rough-looking man scanned the room, his eyes halting momentarily on Stephen and Gilbert, and then knocked back the remains of his ale. He tossed his cup to one of the servants, who saved himself from dropping it by a juggling act, and left. Someone had an accident out of sight in the pantry; heads swiveled at the crash of shattering pottery and there was momentary quiet before the outbreak of thunderous laughter at the guilty servant's misfortune.

"Poor fellow," Gilbert said, leaning over his cup. "He'll be fined for it. Crockery is expensive you know, even the cheap stuff."

"You'd do the same, wouldn't you?" Stephen asked.

Gilbert sighed. "Probably. It's the way of the business, I suppose. At least we don't beat the servants like the stewards on the manor do with their rustics."

"It happens less than you think. They are not completely without rights."

"Yet it happens."

"Yes, it does."

The door to the street burst open, admitting a draft of cold wind that brought expressions of annoyance from those nearest to it, and a spindly man with hair that stood out from his head as if buffeted in a gale.

The apparition peered around the interior, ignoring shouts to close the door. He spotted Stephen and rushed over. His expression was highly agitated, and fearful.

"Lord Attebrook!" cried the fellow, who was the chief groom of the stable across the street. "You must come immediately! Your horse! She got her leg caught in the stall and I fear it's broken!"

Stephen shot to his feet at this news. The prospect that his riding horse had broken a leg was a dire thing to hear. Broken legs could not be mended and meant the loss of the horse and a lot of walking. He darted around the groom who followed closely at his heels.

He burst into the street, which was black soup since his eyes were accustomed to the light. He had taken no more than a step or two before he was aware of dim figures in front of him. Before he could fully register their presence, something struck him a terrible blow in the stomach that drove the breath from his body; it felt like the butt end of a club. He folded like wet laundry, still falling when another blow caught him in the shoulder. Club blows rained down upon his arms, body and legs as he lay curled up, struggling to breathe. For the most part, except for one crack on the cheekbone, they avoided his head, and this told Stephen, although he was capable of only the dimmest thought, that whoever these men were they didn't intend to kill him. It must be robbery.

After Stephen had been thoroughly pummeled, one of his attackers knelt by his head and put his lip's to Stephen's ear. "Stay away from Ingrede Paddoc," said a voice sodden with garlic. "This is your only warning. Disregard it and you'll get something worse."

With that, the attackers faded into the dark. Their footfalls could be heard heading toward the church and they were gone.

Gilbert then was by his side; one of the assailants had restrained him while the others went to work. "Stephen! Are you all right?"

"Do you think they meant to leave me feeling all right?" Stephen wheezed. He sat up and touched the sore cheek. It throbbed but by some miracle it had not broken open and there was no blood. "Nothing's broken, except my pride."

"Plumton's men?" Gilbert said.

"I'd put money on it. I still have my purse and there was that warning. Where's that damned groom?"

The groom had disappeared. It took rousing the stable keeper and securing a lantern to enable them to find him hiding behind stacks of hay in a shed. It was a clever hiding place and only the second spot they looked.

"Please, sir!" the groom implored piteously when Stephen hauled him out of his crevasse by the hair. "Please!"

"You helped them. Why?"

"They threatened me with harm, sir, terrible harm," the groom pleaded. "I had no choice. I know those men. They have no mercy."

"And no money greased your palm?" Stephen said, giving the pathetic fellow a shake.

"Well, sir, I —"

"Give over what they paid you," Stephen snarled.

The groom, after some hesitation, produced two pence from his pouch.

"Not twelve pieces of silver, but I'm sure it was enough," Gilbert said. "But I also think those fellows did threaten violence. What can a little man like him do against that?"

Stephen's lungs worked like bellows, fueling a livid anger, but Gilbert's words diminished his rage, even if only a little so that some rational thought was now possible.

"I suppose you're right," he said.

He gave one of the pennies to the stable keeper for his help in the search and returned the other to the groom.

"Keep your blood money. You'll sleep with my horse tonight and ensure that no real harm comes to her," Stephen said. "I'll need her tomorrow and she better be fit and ready."

Chapter 19

"I should do it. I should go," Gilbert said. They were lying in bed with the covers up to their chins savoring the warmth and each dreading getting up. The room was unheated and cold, as were most upstairs chambers. Dawn had come and there were cocks crowing in the neighboring back gardens. A dog barked. Assorted bumps and thumps shook the house around them; people were already getting up.

"I wonder if they have the fire going yet," Stephen said by way of avoidance and answer.

"I am serious," Gilbert said. "You're in no shape for it, after the beating you've taken. You should look at yourself — bruises everywhere. That one on your cheek is especially nasty, all yellow and black. It looks like it could turn rotten, then we'll have to cut your head off to save you. Take a day or two and rest."

"I'll be fine."

"But what if you're recognized?"

"Only Plumton got a look at me. The others had no idea who they were hitting. It was just a guess that I'd be first out of the inn."

"A canny guess."

"And I'm unlikely to meet Plumton even if he's in residence. How often does a baron dally away time with his villeins?"

"You do."

"I like to see things grow and prosper. From the look of him, Plumton leaves the savoring of such pleasures to his bailiffs and his reeves."

"You're an idiot, that's the last thing I'm going to say."

"Thanks. That's very kind of you."

The road to Worcester Ingrede mentioned wasn't that running down the west side of the Severn but the one to the east, connecting that town and Wribbenhall, the village on the opposite back from Bewdley.

Fortified with a johnny cake and cheese breakfast, Stephen crossed the Severn on the ferry to Wribbenhall and then took the road south. His directions were to stay on this road. It ran smack into Hartley Green where the road struck the one connecting Kidderminster to Worcester.

It was a pleasant ride through forests and prosperous fields until he was about an hour out and he spotted a dust cloud in the distance around the bend in the road. Such a cloud usually signified a group of horsemen. The beating had knocked some caution into his head, and he turned the horse around and galloped to the forest fifty yards back. Once within it, he swerved from the road. He left the horse tied to a tree and worked his way back to the road, taking cover behind a fat oak.

He was not there any time at all when a mounted party came trotting down the road at a brisk pace. Plumton rode at the head of the column and behind him came a couple of knights, some mounted sergeants and one or two squires, eight men in all. He must be off to see Ingrede again. Murderer he might be, but he presented a stirring picture of nobility, sitting well and erect on a powerful stallion. It would be hard to accuse such a man; absolute proof would be necessary since Plumton would enjoy every possible doubt. And there were his political connections to think of. A failed accusation could rebound and impale the accuser. Stephen scanned the faces of all the men. None of them had a flat nose. At least, he didn't think so. He didn't get a perfect look at all of them.

There were three kinds of people who knew everything that happened in a village and everybody in it — the vicar or priest, the blacksmith, and the alewife; the vicar or priest because he saw everyone every Sunday and the churchyard was a hotbed of gossip; the blacksmith because people often hung about the forge to have small articles repaired and conversation naturally ensued; and the alewife for obvious reasons as strong ale loosened tongues. Of the three, the one that would excite the least curiosity when a stranger dropped in was the alewife. Hartley Green was on the road to Worcester so it got its fair share of travelers stopping off for a drink and perhaps a bit of rest.

Stephen passed the manor house before he reached the village. It was a tall stone house with a blue tile roof, surrounded by a moat choking with water plants and a low wall. He kept his head down in apprehension even though it seemed unlikely that anyone there — the porter lingered in the gate to watch him with what appeared to be some suspicion — would recognize him. He remembered the man who had left the Bewdley inn just before the groom raised the false alarm about his horse and wondered if at least some of Plumton's men knew his face.

The village alehouse was across the road from the church, identifiable by a broom hung over the door. No one was on the benches outside the house nor visible in the garden. As Stephen tied his horse to a post in the yard, he heard a child's voice singing. He went into the house.

There was a woman seated on a bench nursing a baby while a girl of about four fell silent and tucked the rag doll that had been her audience under an arm.

"Mum!" the little girl said and pointed at him.

The woman turned to Stephen with surprise on her face.

"I'm sorry," Stephen said. "I thought you were open for business."

"Ah," the woman said removing the child from her breast. "I forgot to take the broom down last night." The hanging broom was the sign that the alehouse was doing business. She put the child in a cradle. "Well, you might as well stay for the custom. What will you have the small ale or the small ale?"

Stephen smiled. "I'll have the small ale then. Do you mind if I sit down?"

The alewife waved at the bench across the fire. "Addie, fetch the gentleman a cup." She asked as the child ran for the cup, "What in Saint Agatha's name happened to you?"

"I fell off a horse."

"And landed head first without breaking your neck? You are a lucky one."

"Where are you traveling?" the alewife asked as she handed Stephen a full cup.

"Worcester," Stephen said.

"Ah, it is a fair piece yet."

"And how far is that?"

"Another nine miles or so, or so they tell me. I've never been there."

"It is a fine town, though it was roughly handled by the barons' men last year."

"I heard that quite a bit of it burned." The woman shuddered. "Wherever armies go, the little people suffer. Thank God none has come here."

"That's true. What place is this?"

"Hartley Green."

"Hartley Green, you say?" Stephen said as if he was surprised to hear this. "I know a fellow who said he was from Hartley Green. He owes me a bit of money — a lost wager that he failed to pay up on."

"What's his name? I'm sure I know him."

"Everyone comes here, eh?"

The woman chuckled. "Even the boys from the manor house."

"The lot of them, I'll bet." —he hoped — "I heard this was a baron's home."

"Lord Plumton," she said. "So, what's this fellow's name?"

"He called himself Tom."

"Toms are as common around here as sheep. I'll need to know more."

"Well, this fellow, he has the look of a soldier. A hard man. I think he might be a sergeant for the baron. He has a scar here," Stephen indicated the spot on the left side of his mouth, "and rather squashed nose, flattened and crooked, as if he had been a boxer."

The alewife shook her head. "We've no one named Tom like that."

"Nor anyone at all?"

"Not a one."

"And you know them all …."

"Every single one, down to the grooms and gardeners and the poor fellows who burn out the privies. Did this Tom owe you a great deal of money?"

"A fair amount."

"It sounds like you've been had. Tom probably wasn't his real name and he wasn't from around here."

"It seems I may have been." He had been had by his hope that this single inquiry would solve the murder. But nothing was ever simple. Flat-nose could be a man quartered at another of Plumton's manors or even a hired assassin. And if flat nose was such a man, Stephen would never find him.

Chapter 20

Gilbert Wistwode spent a couple of hours in the morning after Stephen's departure playing backgammon in the hall. It might have been profitable, since it was a popular gambling game and in his own opinion he was quite good at it, but he had to play against himself since the hall was deserted as all the guests left for their days' destinations. After a while, when the joy of victory, the pain of defeat and the boredom of solitude grew too great, he gave up his bench and the cushion the innkeeper had grudgingly provided and went out to explore the town.

He had no sooner stepped into the street than a party of horsemen came trotting up from the ferry, scattering everyone in their path. Gilbert flattened himself against the inn, bumping his head painfully on a shutter. But he was not so dazed that he failed to recognize the black-haired aristocrat both he and Stephen had passed outside the house of Ingrede Paddoc — Baron Richard Plumton.

The party halted just down the street at another inn. Plumton and his men dismounted. Several of his men led the horses off to the nearby stable while the rest entered the inn. The baron marched back toward the river and vanished around the corner.

Gilbert's feet took him down the street to the ferry, which he watched cross and recross with cargoes of people, carts, horses and the occasional oxen. Boats on the river came and went, stopping at the quay to load and unload. Down by the end he noticed a gathering of swans and ducks. This gave him an idea. He went up to a bun shop and bought a two-day old loaf that was as hard as a stone and ready to feed to the pigs. Then he went to the end of the quay, dangled his legs over the edge and broke off pieces of the loaf, which he tossed into the river. The swans were aggressively eager for it and it was not long before he had a crowd of them beneath his feet. The ducks, more reserved and dignified, patrolled the edges to receive those bits Gilbert was able to throw beyond the swans.

It wasn't long before the loaf was gone. The swans paddled about hoping for more, but when nothing was forthcoming, lost interest and went back to searching the depths for food.

An hour passed and Plumton emerged from Ingrede's house. Whatever words passed between them were not satisfactory. Plumton's face was a study in furious disappointment. He stalked up the quay and disappeared into Lode Street, the image of a man used to getting what he wanted and not used to being denied. He looked, to Gilbert, precisely like a man who might commit murder.

Gilbert was about to rise when a young boy came onto the quay. He had a fishing pole, which he hung over a vacant space between two boats and dropped his line into the river. It soon became clear that the boy's attention was not on his fishing pole but on Ingrede's house. He was watching to see who might go there next, a hired spy for Plumton, no doubt.

It was at that moment that Gilbert remembered something Stephen had forgotten to do; to be charitable, Gilbert had not thought of it either, as he should have done when they were talking with Ingrede. It was an important thing, so significant a question that he was appalled that neither of them remembered to ask it. His impulse was to rush to Ingrede's house and blurt it out. But the spy made him check this impulse. He didn't want to be seen going to her house. He would be mistaken for a messenger of another doting suitor. Something worse than last night's beating might come of it.

So caution drove him up Lode Street and past the church to the spot where the three roads leading out of town came together. There were more houses on the stems of these departing streets, but they ended a short distance away. He went up the one heading northward to the last house. An apple orchard occupied the neighboring ground. Commonly, such orchards were fenced, but this was not, so Gilbert felt less guilty of trespassing as he slipped through the orchard to the back gardens of the houses fronting the quay. There was no actual reason to feel that way, but there it was. Men were not always rational. Still, he did listen for a shout and was prepared with an explanation.

He came to a wicker fence separating the back gardens from the orchard and counted the houses to ensure he got the right one. Then, careful not to break the fence, for wicker fences were flimsy and his substantial weight would collapse it, he tumbled ungracefully over it, avoiding an impact with his head by mere chance.

Picking himself up and scanning the surroundings for onlookers, he dusted away imaginary dust and crossed to the back door.

He knocked on the door and stood back to wait.

Shortly, the door opened and a servant girl regarded him with suspicion.

"Take one step forward and I will scream," she said. Strangers did not ordinarily come to the back door for any honest purpose.

"My dear," Gilbert said hurriedly, "I pose no threat nor mean any offense. I need to speak with the mistress, and the house is watched. I do not want to be seen."

"Oh, yes, Hankin," the girl said. "We know."

"There was some trouble with the baron last night and I want to avoid a repeat performance. I suspect that Baron Plumton has employed him to note the comings and goings."

"Clever of you to figure that out. Whose love letter have you brought? Who are you here for? Leuon? Erley? Galant?"

For an eternal instant, Gilbert could not believe what he had heard. "Wait — what did you say? Galant? Would that be Philip Galant?"

"What is it, Alyn?" Ingrede's faint voice called from the interior of the house.

"A bothersome man, mistress," Alyn called back over her shoulder.

"At the back door?" Ingrede said.

"Another tiresome love poem or something, mistress," Alyn said.

"Oh, send him away," Ingrede said. "And let him keep his letter."

"You heard the mistress," Alyn said to Gilbert. "Go away and don't bother this house again."

"Young lady —" Gilbert got out by way of explanation, but Alyn was having none of it. She pushed Gilbert back with the palm of her hand.

But she had not taken Gilbert's rather substantial bulk into account; although he was short, he was solid. So he no more than rocked a bit.

At this failure, Alyn threw her weight against the door to close it on him.

Gilbert threw his own shoulder against the door to prevent this and managed to insert one foot between the door and its jam. He immediately regretted this because the pain of the closing door on his old foot was more than he was willing to endure. Alyn was a slight girl, but in an emergency had proved more capable than you would expect.

"Bertrand! Help! An intruder!" Alyn cried as she redoubled her efforts to close the door, Gilbert's foot notwithstanding.

At this point, Gilbert's efforts were aimed at recovering his foot before it might be broken or pinched off his leg, efforts made more frantic by the prospect of Bertrand adding his muscular bulk to the attack.

"If you will just release my foot, I will go!" Gilbert gasped.

He saw a vague shape moving beyond the crack in the door and realized his fate was sealed and that he might be maimed for life, perhaps with half a foot remaining just like Stephen.

But abruptly the pressure withdrew. The door opened. Bertrand stood there, all dark menace.

"You," he said. "What are you doing here?"

"I came back to ask a question of the mistress," Gilbert panted. "But perhaps you two might have the answer."

Bertrand grasped Gilbert's coat, lifted him off his feet and drew him into the house.

"You're letting him in?" Alyn asked, aghast.

"He's not here on behalf of one of those lovesick idiots. He was here yesterday with that deputy sheriff," Bertrand said. "They are looking into William Griffin's death."

"Well, dear Lord," Alyn said. "Why didn't you say so straightaway. It would have saved a lot of trouble."

"And my poor foot, I suppose," Gilbert said. "I hope you have not mangled it beyond repair."

Bertrand thrust Gilbert into the hall, where Ingrede was seated by the fire with another servant girl. They were making a dress as if they were a pair of tailors, a very nice dress by the look of what had been done.

Ingrede set her hands in her lap, mindful of the needle in her fingers. "Well, Master Wistwode? What brings you here?"

Gilbert took a deep breath to calm his racing heart. "We forgot to ask you a question. We were so focused on one man that we gave no thought to the others." He wondered why he had admitted this mistake out loud.

"And?"

"Your servant Alyn mentioned three others who are vying for your hand."

"Yes, John Erley, Philip Galant and Miles Leuon," Ingrede said. "Although 'vying for my hand' is an exaggeration. All are trying to make a mistress of me. I am not well-born enough for a wife."

"Would that be Philip Galant of Upper Arley?" Gilbert said.

"It would."

"Has he been in contact with you since Lord Griffin died?"

"He has indeed. He's come twice himself and sent letters by messengers on four occasions. Don't tell me he could be a suspect. Do you really think he killed his own cousin? Over me?"

"I have only suspicions, mistress," Gilbert said. "There is rather a sad absence of proof everywhere we look. But if he was jealous of Lord Griffin, that provides a substantial reason to consider him a suspect."

"Well," Ingrede sighed, "Philip and Richard *are* two peas in a pod. Both like getting their way and are unhappy at being thwarted. But I cannot see him as a murderer. Not of his own kin."

"No," Gilbert said heavily. "I suppose you're right."

"We heard about what happened to Sir Stephen," Ingrede said. "I'm sure that Richard was behind it. You should look to him before all others."

Gilbert nodded. "I'm sorry to have troubled you. If someone could show me out — by the back way? I don't want to give Baron Plumton cause to act again."

Chapter 21

Stephen returned to Bewdley by way of Kidderminster instead of the way he had come to avoid the chance that he might meet Plumton. It was a much longer journey and taxed him more than he expected. He ached abominably from the beating, and he went to bed as soon as he had something to eat.

He did not rise at dawn like everyone else at the inn but remained in bed, resisting Gilbert's suggestion that he at least come down for breakfast.

"Come on," Gilbert said. "You should get some food into you. Aren't we going home today? We've done all we could do."

"Maybe tomorrow, we'll go," Stephen said, his face in the pillow. He was defeated and he did not like having to admit it.

Gilbert shrugged and left him.

At loose ends after breakfast, Gilbert bought three old hard loaves of bread and descended to the quay. Hankin the watchboy was already on station with his fishing pole, but paid Gilbert no attention. The swans and ducks were glad to see him and swarmed about (the swans anyway) to the annoyance of some watermen intent on tying up where the swan mob had collected. After some choice words from the watermen, Gilbert moved to the end of the quay.

The loaves distributed, Gilbert dusted the crumbs from his coat and headed back up Lode Street. Halfway to the inn, he passed two men leading three horses, two for riding and one packhorse, heading in the opposite direction. Such a sight was as ordinary as could be in most circumstances, but one thing about one of the men so startled Gilbert that he stopped short and gaped.

One of those men had a crooked left arm, bent about six inches above the wrist. He was square built, with squinty eyes and a short brown beard. At the moment he was an angry man, muttering about being sent on a stupid errand and why couldn't the lady have sent someone else.

The crooked armed man couldn't help noticing Gilbert's stare and, suspecting what he was gawping at, since deformities always drew attention and none of it favorable, he withdrew the damaged arm under the fold of his cloak.

"What're you looking at, you fat little bastard?" the crooked armed man spat.

"Oh, oh, why, nothing!" Gilbert stammered.

The crooked armed man grasped Gilbert's cloak with his good right hand and drew their faces close together. "Nothing, you say, you piebald liar," the crooked armed man snarled. "Laugh or make fun, and I'll cut your tongue out."

"Oh, I would never think of such a thing! Why, one of my best friends hasn't any legs. I would never make fun."

"Phew!" the crooked armed man uttered and pushed Gilbert away so violently that he stumbled and fell. "You take me for a fool."

He spun away and he and his companion continued on a few houses to a potter's shop. Crooked-arm pounded on the counter and shouted through the window for someone to attend him and hurry up about it.

It was some moments before a rattled Gilbert was able to scramble to his feet. He walked fast, suppressing an urge to run, back to his inn, and clambered up the stairs.

"Stephen! Get up! Quick!" Gilbert panted as he shook Stephen's shoulder. "I've just seen a man with a crooked arm — just as Ida described."

Stephen sat up, rubbing his head as if to dispel cobwebs that confused his thoughts. "What?"

"I said, I've just seen a crooked armed man! He may be the one Ida heard about!"

"Fat chance, the way our luck is running," Stephen said.

"Well, you'll never know for sure if you just lie there."

"All right, all right."

They hurried out together and stood in the inn's doorway. Gilbert pointed the pair out. They were taking several glazed pieces of pottery through the open shop window and packing them in leather bags on either side of the packhorse. The crooked wrist of one of them was clearly visible and could not be missed. The men mounted and turned up the street, heading toward the church.

"Damn me," Stephen said.

"They're getting away," Gilbert said.

"Not yet, they're not."

Stephen dashed back to their chamber, collected his sword and shield, and raced back to the hall, practically sliding down the banister in his haste. He had made quick time, for the two men were still in sight, just disappearing around a bend to the right.

He ran across the street to the stable, where he shouted at one of the grooms to fetch his palfrey while he gathered his saddle, girth and bridle. The two of them tacked up the horse in quick time, and Stephen trotted out to the street, knocking over a woman bearing a load of laundry on her head at the gate. The laundry spilled and Stephen burst into a gallop, the laundress' angry cries filling the air.

Behind the church where the three roads leaving town came together, he could not see them. He called to a carter if he had seen two men leading a packhorse, and the carter pointed to the road leading northward.

Stephen galloped on and soon the two men came into sight. He slowed sharply, fearful that they might have heard him coming, but neither man looked back. He let them get well ahead. He didn't want to be noticed. There were many bends in this road and he lost sight of them from time to time, but he refused to allow himself to rush even though he was worried that they might turn off at any moment and he'd lose them.

The undulating fields about Bewdley gave way to the thick forest of the Wyre after half a mile and there he almost rode up upon them, for they had halted to water their horses at the ford of a little brook running down to the Severn. Stephen leaped from his horse and led her into the forest to avoid being seen, then he peered around a tree to watch.

There was a Crooked Man

Onward they plodded, slow and steady, mindful of the fragility of the pottery, Stephen holding back as far as he dared, although this deep in the forest there were no tracks leading away from the road. They went by the spot where William Griffin and his groom were murdered and shortly after that they came to the lane to Fox Hall. Stephen's targets took the turn and ambled down the track. After perhaps half a mile the forest surrendered to the fields surrounding the village. They were flat and open and Stephen did not dare follow here. They were clearly headed toward Fox Hall since the track went nowhere else ... except the path beyond led to Upper Arley.

Stephen swung the horse right and hurried along the verge of the forest enclosing the fields of Fox Hall, swerving about trees and ducking branches in his haste. Now and then he glimpsed people working in the fields, sowing and harrowing, crows and flocks of blackbirds orbiting about looking for an opportunity to steal some sustenance. Occasionally Stephen thought that he might have been seen, but he was so focused on reaching the ferry before Crooked-arm that he didn't care about the fact that the sight of such a stranger riding the verge of the forest was sure to be reported to the steward.

At long last, after much twisting and turning, face lashed and scratched, the bruise on his cheek thundering, he burst into a meadow above the Severn. Cattle dotted the meadow and hardly paid any notice as Stephen pushed the horse into a gallop on the last quarter mile.

There was no place to hide in this meadow and observe the ferry landing but a copse two-hundred yards from it. Stephen dismounted, hoping to remain unnoticed, and kept his eyes on the road up the slope. He was sure he had beaten them. They should appear at any moment.

Yet a quarter hour, then a half hour and finally a whole hour went by without anyone visible on the road and nothing happening at the ferry.

It was only then that he realized Crooked-arm's destination was Fox Hall after all. But that made sense in its own way.

The thing to do now was to return to Bewdley and then hurry to Alditheley for the collection of a sheriff's party of mounted sergeants to arrest Crooked-arm. And yet he knew there was more to learn and he needed to know it as much as he needed to breathe.

Stephen remounted, crossed the meadow to the road and descended to the ferry landing.

He pulled the red flag from its box and waved it over his head. Presently someone on the opposite bank spotted him and shouted, "Hold on! We'll be over directly."

Five men came trotting down from the village and clambered into the ferryboat. They pushed off from the bank and rowed across the Severn. The boat grounded at Stephen's feet with a crunch.

The same steersman who had captained the boat before stood in the stern, arm on his steering oar. He recognized Stephen and said, "Why've you not stopped at Fox Hall, sir? Lord Galant is there. Not in Upper Arley."

"Because I have a few questions, and I think you should be able to answer them," Stephen said.

"Questions? What questions?"

"Is there a man in Lord Galant's service with a crooked left arm?"

"Yea, that's Beck," the steersman said, puzzled and with a hint of disapproval.

"And also a man with a flattened nose and a scar here?" Stephen indicated the spot on his lip.

"That's Bate. What do you want with them?" the steersman asked.

"Bad lot, that's what they are," muttered one of the oarsmen.

"Bullies," agreed another in a low voice.

"I wonder if they've finally stepped in it," a third one said.

"Did you take Beck and Bate across from Upper Arley on the last day of February?" Stephen asked.

"Yea, and Lord Griffin, too," the steersman said. "And we brought them back again later in the day."

"And again, perhaps on the following Monday?" Stephen asked. "All of them?"

The steersman nodded, still perplexed.

"And I guess that would have been early," Stephen said.

"Right, at first light, it was," the steersman said.

"And you returned them to Upper Arley, when, Tuesday afternoon?"

"That's right. What is this about?"

"Just my idle curiosity," Stephen answered. He tossed three pennies into the boat. "For your trouble."

Before Stephen turned away, he asked, "What's your name, by the way?"

"Tenney Redette," the steersman said.

"Pleased to meet you."

"I am likewise, sir," Redette said.

You may not be once I've wrung your testimony from you at trial, Stephen thought to himself.

The road from the ferry landing ran along the riverbank for a short distance, then turned right and headed uphill back toward Fox Hall. As Stephen reached the turn, he noticed a modest lane leading southward along the riverbank. He called to the rivermen, who were halfway across, "Where does this lane lead?"

"To Bewdley!" Redette called back. "It follows the line of the river and it's a quicker way from here than going through Fox Hall, if that's in your mind! Say, didn't you come that way?"

Stephen waved his thanks and turned into the lane. If the steersman was speaking truly, it would be a shorter journey and not involve the risk of returning around Fox Hall. He did not want to alert Galant or his ruffians that he was on to them; the arrest should come as a surprise.

Beck Cruker found Philip Galant at the Fox Hall dovecote. The cote was a dome-shaped stone shell with slits above a man's head for the birds to fly in and out. It was a common practice for manors to keep birds, for doves and their eggs could be good eating. The birds nested in niches all around the inside. Periodically, it needed mucking out for the birds produced a prodigious amount of feces, which could be sold at a good profit for fertilizer. It was an awful job, however. The inside of the cote stank worse than a privy. People working inside were known to faint from the stench, so they were only able to work for a short time before having to be relieved; at least two teams of men were needed to get the job done. It was not a popular job and the reeve had difficulty finding villeins who would do the work, so Galant had to go around himself and frightened the rustics.

"My lord!" Cruker leaped from his horse.

"What have you done with the pots?" Galant cut him off.

"James has taken them to the house, lord. I had to come straight here myself. I've news. That deputy sheriff followed me from Bewdley. I saw him plainly on the road. And I saw that little fat friend of his on the street. That's what alerted me to keep a good lookout behind us."

"He followed you? Attebrook followed you? Here?" Galant said, keeping his voice calm, although the news sent tremors of apprehension through him. He had feared something like this might happen eventually. He had been careful, but they said Attebrook was a demon at finding things out. Only yesterday they had news that the sheriff, led by Attebrook, had arrested the gang responsible for the terrible murders in Staffordshire and Shropshire. It would take them only a turn of the screw to determine that the gang had not killed William Griffin, and then they would cast about for another culprit.

"Yes, sir," Cruker gulped. "And I recognized the horse — from, well, you know."

"Are you sure it was that man?"

"Taller than most, lean, black hair. I got a good look at him before. I'm sure it was him."

"We must keep —" A thought intruded and Galant let the sentence die. There was no reason to connect Cruker with William's death, but there was to Red John's. There had been a witness after all, that urchin girl they hauled from the stairwell and who got away before they could silence her. Attebrook must have found her somehow and talked to her. But to reassure Cruker, he went on, "We must think clearly about what to do about this. There is a way to deal with it. Come."

They headed toward the manor house but they had got only a few steps when a boy came riding in from the fields.

"Lord, Rufus sent me to say that we saw a man riding in the woods at the east meadow. He thinks it's a poacher."

"In the east forest?" Galant said.

"Yes, lord."

"Where was a going? Did anyone see?"

"He was riding north, lord. Toward the river."

Galant felt as if he had been struck by a bolt of lightning. Attebrook wasn't going toward the river — he was going to the ferry. He meant to ask that jovial loose-lip Tenney Redette who he had carried across the river and when!

The tremor of enlightenment gave way to a shiver of panic. Attebrook would be able to connect him personally with Cruker and Rodes on the days that William and John had died, a connection that demonstrated their opportunity; it wouldn't be proof of guilt by itself, but it was enough to support an arrest. And a determined sheriff would grind a confession out of him and the others once they were in hold. He might have been able to brazen out an accusation against either of them alone — if he got them away and in hiding — by claiming they must have been hired by another, like Plumton, but that strategy would fail before Redette's testimony. And there were the others, the oarsmen, to think about. He couldn't silence them all. But he could stop Attebrook and the threat would end there; it was unlikely that anyone else would be clever enough to think of the ferry. He would have it done properly this time.

But how to do it? The sooner the better. But how? He struggled with the problem and then it came to him in another flash of enlightenment. Attebrook would take the river lane back to Bewdley. It was shorter and would not expose him to the eyes of Fox Hall. Several secret forest paths led to convenient spots they could reach before Attebrook if he was not in a hurry to return to Bewdley. There was yet hope.

"Fetch my weapons and your own. And find Rodes right away," Galant snapped. "I'll see to our horses."

Chapter 22

The lane was a mere cart track rather than a proper road but it was well-traveled so it was easy to follow. The reason for its heavy use lay in the fact that it was five or more miles from Upper Arley to Kidderminster by the roads east of the Severn, but it was only three and a bit to Bewdley. Although Bewdley was smaller, it was also a market town that competed favorably with its larger sister — in fact it often offered goods at cheaper prices because of its proximity to the river.

During the pursuit Stephen had refused to entertain any feelings about the effects of the beating. But now that one, no two, riddles had been solved, he was exhausted. His head throbbed and the body aches returned. He pointed the horse down the lane. At first Stephen insisted on a trot despite the punishing nature of that gait until they reached the forest that fell down the slopes to the river. Then he let the mare slow to a walk, for her sake as well as his. The lane ran along the riverbank, the stream's brown water visible though the yet-leafless trees, which patiently waited for the arrival of spring. Sometimes the path ran within an arm's reach of the water; sometimes it wandered farther away, but he was never out of sight of it.

At first river and lane ran southward, the oval medallion of the sun, pale and heatless, struggling to penetrate a low roof of clouds on Stephen's left. Before long, the river and lane bent eastward for almost a mile, then curled southward again.

It was blissfully serene; silent except for the burble of the river flowing over shallows, the flutter of birds, and the faint rattling of tree branches stirred by a gentle breeze. It was lulling and Stephen's eyelids grew heavy. He was tempted to sleep in the saddle; he had done so before many times in the past. It was a relief to know that all his finder work was done. All he had to do now was report to Alditheley.

He was nodding off, in fact, when the horse's gait suddenly changed, the thing that always woke up a sleeping rider.

The mare snorted and sniffed vigorously, her ears back, and she swung to the right — all signs she was alarmed about something. Horses will spook at just about anything, a falling leaf, an unexpected obstacle in the road, a person making a sudden appearance or approach. Stephen had seen a horse spook and throw its rider when a woman blew her nose on a handkerchief. So often such alerts meant nothing except to a horse.

But he was awake now, jolted back to reality, and could not help but turn himself to see if anything was truly the matter.

Three men had risen from the ground, old brown leaves falling from their coats or still clinging to them no more than ten yards away. Two held bows and one a crossbow.

Stephen recognized them immediately — Philip Galant, the crooked-armed Beck Cruker, and flat-nosed Bate de Rodes.

As Stephen swung round, they all shot at the same time. And it was that swing, the horse's decision and not his, that saved him from instant death. For the momentum of the swing brought around the shield hanging on its strap about his neck, and by sheer reflex he was able to continue its motion to cover his front. Both arrows struck the shield with sharp blows, the heads penetrating the wood, producing a small spray of splinters, and nearly piercing his left forearm.

But it was the crossbow bolt that did the most harm. It slammed into the upper right corner of the shield, driving it back, and at the same time the bolt head came clear through. The violent force of the impact drove the bolt into Stephen's upper chest and knocked him out of the saddle.

He had fallen many times from horses before and again reflexes saved him from fatal injury, for he twisted in flight and landed on his side rather than flat on his back. The bolt pinned Stephen to the shield but the fall dislodged it, but he had no time to spare for the wound when his killers were so close. They would be on him with their swords in only a moment.

The mare, bless her, bolted at the attack, but instead of swinging about to flee, crashed through the attackers, sending Galant and Rodes diving out of the way.

Stephen forced himself to his feet. He drew his sword, feeling the wound in his chest but unhampered by it as yet, and charged.

Cruker had a foot in the stirrup of the crossbow and was frantically trying to draw back the string to reload when Stephen cut him down through the crown of his head. The sword's blade halted at Cruker's teeth. Stephen jerked the blade free and turned to Galant and Rodes as Cruker toppled backwards like a falling tree.

Galant and Rodes had no time to use their fallen bows. They drew their own swords and brought around their own shields.

The fighters regarded each other, chests heaving.

Then Galant and Rodes exchanged looks. "Get him!" Galant cried.

And they rushed together at Stephen.

Obviously, they hoped that their shields and coordinated rush would protect them from any blow Stephen might deliver before he was knocked off his feet and finished on the ground. It was, in fact, the way two men should assault a lone man; both at once rather than one at a time.

But Stephen sidestepped far to his right as they came together and, pivoting on his out-stretched right foot (thank God it was his good one), he slashed downward as hard as he could at the back of Rodes' head. Rodes dove face down into the leaves and was still.

Galant, his charge frustrated, turned to face Stephen alone. His eyes flicked to the dead men and the light of fear began to shine in them. He hefted his sword, the point bobbing up and down in Stephen's direction, but he did not come on. It was clear he was thinking about what to do now, when he was alone. And his face betrayed the fact he had no confidence in victory. He was no fighting man and it was easier to shoot a man in the back than to trade blows face to face.

He took one step back, then another. He turned and ran into the forest.

Stephen was too spent to chase him. His chest throbbed, every part of him throbbed. And he found he could barely breathe. The world seemed dim and wobbly. He thought that if he took a single step, he would fall. The rustle of Galant's footsteps faded, shortly followed by the unmistakable crash of a horse dashing away.

Chapter 23

Stephen reached Bewdley after a long, painful ride. He had been grievously wounded before — the loss of his left foot and the subsequent infection that nearly killed him were still fresh in his memory. But the harm to his shoulder hurt more than all but that one, and spasms of agony pulsed with each beat of his heart. It did not bleed much but that was no indication that great harm hadn't been done by the impact or the wrenching away of the bolt.

At last, the horse turned into Lode Street as if she knew where to go, and Stephen, slumped in the saddle, patted her neck in thanks. She was a good girl and had served him well.

People stared at him as he rode down Lode Street, wobbling in the saddle, for he knew he must look a sight. He had lost his hat in the fight and had not recovered it, and he was covered with a patchwork of leaves clinging to his cloak and hair, which was in disarray. People murmured and pointed, and he heard at least one of them mention Plumton's name.

He slipped from the saddle in the stable yard, and dropped the reins, and staggered to a bench by the door. A pair of young grooms, alerted to his arrival by the sound of hoof beats, strolled out of the barn. Their mouths dropped to the ground at the sight of him.

"Lord!" one of them cried. "What's happened!"

"A bit of bad luck," Stephen said, easing back against the wall of the barn. "Please see that my girl is taken care of, will you? Water and an extra ration of oats. Then sweet hay."

One of the boys took up the mare's reins and led her into the barn. The other said, "I'll fetch your servant."

Stephen nodded. He didn't seem to have the strength left to contradict the boy that Gilbert wasn't his servant.

Gilbert came rushing in, the groom at his heels, cloak flapping about him like a set of wings. He sat beside Stephen, removing his hand from the wound. "What in God's name have you done to yourself now?"

"It was Galant all along," Stephen said. He told Gilbert what he had learned and surmised as Gilbert pulled his coat and shirt away so he could see the wound more closely.

His fingers about the hole, which was high on the chest just beneath the right collarbone, Gilbert said, "Can you take a deep breath?"

Stephen sucked in a load of air, and let it out.

"Well, at least the bolt didn't pierce your lung. Your shield must have absorbed the impact. In fact, I think the thing is rather shallow."

"You're telling me it's only a flesh wound?"

"Probably," Gilbert said, pressing the edges of it. He could only know how deep it was by setting a finger in it, but of course, that would not be possible. "You may live after all."

"There are some who would be disappointed."

"You hush and say nothing of the sort."

Stephen pushed Gilbert's hands away and tried to sit forward. "We need to alert the sheriff right away. There's no time to waste."

"Waste?" Gilbert said, refusing to let his hands be displaced or for Stephen to sit forward. "What do you mean? Ride for Ludlow, or even Shrewsbury, right now? You're hardly in condition to walk across the street. Haste is not needed. I doubt Galant will be within twenty miles by sundown."

"I suppose you're right," Stephen said. "But we still have to let Alditheley know."

"Of course, we do. But he can learn of what's happened by letter. You've done what was required. That's enough. Now, let's get you to bed. That's where you ought to be. Not in the saddle, or on this bench."

Despite what Gilbert said about the minor nature of Stephen's wound, he refused to allow Stephen to walk to the inn. He had a litter brought and Stephen carried to his bedchamber by grooms and servants of the stable. They got him as far as the stairway, and he had to climb it without help, but he managed, though slowly, with Gilbert right behind, ready to catch him if he stumbled or fell.

Bewdley was too small to have its own physician, but there was the apothecary, who treated wounds on the side, and he fussed over Stephen, cleansing it with a dosage of sour wine and applying smelly poultices that reeked vaguely of mustard and onion and other things unpleasant. Even minor wounds, assuming that this one was minor, ran the risk of infection; indeed, infection killed more wounded men than the wound itself. Everyone knew the story of how King Richard had died: shot with a crossbow bolt which was successfully extracted, only to have infection carry him off. And he had been a strong man in his prime. Poultices were supposed to be a shield against this fate, but they did not always work.

Gilbert wrote a report to Alditheley but in the meantime, because there was some uncertainty whether the ambush occurred in Worcestershire or Shropshire, the Worcestershire sheriff's bailiff and a few of his men rode out to the river path to have a look at the bodies of Rodes and Cruker. He determined that the ambush occurred in that little finger of Staffordshire that poked across the Severn, to his relief, as that relieved him of having to do anything meaningful about it. However, he left one man to guard the corpses and dispatched another to Stourton to inform Richard Deme. His messenger crossed the Severn at Upper Arley and, when he returned, reported that Philip Galant was neither there nor at Fox Hall; he had left all of a sudden without giving any explanation.

Stephen had several visitors over the next few days. Some were from the town, often luminaries and distinguished merchants, who popped a head in to express their condolences and thanks for ridding the country of some dreadful murderers — living on their own doorsteps! Others were nondescript people who uttered the same words, until Gilbert put a stop to all the indiscriminate visiting by strangers.

"I think the innkeeper's letting them see you for a fee," Gilbert said as he shooed the last of them away.

Ingrede Paddoc came by to see how he was doing, and seemed very sincere about it. She told him she was planning to leave town in a few days for Bristol, where she had an aunt who had agreed to give her shelter from the attentions of her suitors.

A cousin of Will Thumper who lived in the area also called. His interest was more to verify that there would be no reward forthcoming than to establish that Stephen had not yet perished — "I knew well that rascal Cruker, crooked-arm as you called him; I had just sent word to my cousin, too, when I heard you had killed him. Are you sure there's nothing you can do about our efforts? They have been substantial."

"I'm afraid not," Stephen said. He went on to explain that Galant was the one who had put up the reward, and since he was one of the murderers and had since vanished, it was hard to see where any reward might come from.

Godric Carter came two days after the ambush. He mentioned that he would return to Ludlow the next day with a load of salted herring. So it came about that he had a passenger nestled among the barrels and a few random sacks.

Gilbert objected to this from the time he heard of it until at least half an hour after they set out. "You're in no shape to travel! If you die on the way, it will be your own doing. Not mine!"

Stephen called out, "Godric! If I die on the way, tell my wife that it was my doing, not Gilbert's. That way she'll flay my corpse rather than his."

"Right, sir," Godric said. "But he's right. You should stay a few extra days to get your strength back. That's a nasty wound you've got."

"If I'm to die, then I'd rather die in my own house," Stephen said. "Now, what's the matter with those nags you've got. Can't they go any faster?"

"Not if you don't want to be shaken and battered to death, sir," Godric said. "Bad roads make a hard bed, you know."

It was another four days before Ida let Stephen come downstairs and eat in the hall with everyone else. It would be his first actual meal. A diet of broth, even if it was deemed good for his health, didn't qualify as a meal in his judgment. The physician had come by as he did every day to check the wound and change the poultice and had remarked that it had closed up nicely with no sign of infection. If Stephen refrained from riding horses and other strenuous activities for another week, he could be pronounced cured. Stephen used this opinion to overcome Ida's resistance to him leaving the chamber; a bedchamber was as confining as a gaol cell, the bed an excruciating rack.

The evening of his release from confinement sparked a celebration. Joan produced a luscious roast beef, fried apples, and assorted pies, a lot of work for a supper.

Afterward, Stephen, Ida, Harry, Joan and Sarah remained at the table. The boys and Wymar battled with wooden swords about the hearth as the fire burned low and the hall fell into dimness. The single candle on the table struggled to light the room.

"What I don't understand is how this Cruker, this crooked arm, led you to guess that Galant was behind the deaths of both William Griffin and Red John," Ida said.

Stephen paused a long time before answering. "I should have guessed sooner, much sooner," he said at last. "But I was so certain that the Harvington bunch killed William Griffin that I didn't consider all the evidence. William's horses weren't taken. The Harvington boys' primary target was the horses, because they could be sold for a great deal of money. Then there was that fine leather bottle we found at the death site. It wasn't the sort of item a rustic would buy. It cost quite a bit."

"Couldn't they have afforded such a thing from all their ill-got gains?" Harry asked.

"Possibly, yes."

"So there's no reason to fault you for being your usual slow self," Harry said.

"You're not helping me feel any better."

"That's Ida's job," Harry said.

"What finally led you to suspect Galant?" Ida said. "It would be easy to connect him with Red John's death — crooked-arm led you directly to him. And there's the fact that Red John must have known his killer. He unlocked his door for them and provided them with wine, as he would do for his cousin. But William Griffin?"

"Ultimately, apart from the horses, it was the fact the Harvington gang didn't use crossbows. The two men who ambushed me and Gilbert had a crossbow and that was only a few miles from Upper Arley. It would have been easy to set up an ambush. There was at least an hour's delay before we departed. And there was the motive. Galant wanted Ingrede but William offered her marriage, taking her off the board. He was enraged. That may explain why William was so disfigured."

Joan stirred the contents of her cup. "Isn't it simpler to think that Galant killed both Red John and his brother to get Fox Hall Manor? That Ingrede had nothing to do with it? I am sure Ingrede is a prize, but surely she isn't the only one in the county. Why kill for her?"

"We'll never know Galant's motives until we catch him," Stephen said.

"Unless you catch him," Harry said.

"Unless we catch him," Stephen conceded. "But I think his plan initially was to eliminate his most serious rival for Ingrede Paddoc's hand."

"But you said that he didn't want to marry her," Ida said.

"No, but he wanted to possess her," Stephen said. "Pride and jealousy are as powerful a motive as greed."

"How could he think he had any chance of success?" Ida said. "Ingrede sounds like a woman of firm mind."

"Some men are fools," Sarah said.

"I'd say all, but for one or two I know of," Joan said.

"You better be talking about me," Harry said.

"Of course, I am, love," Joan said. She shifted her baby from one arm to the other.

"But if the aim was to clear the field for Ingrede, why kill Red John?" Ida said.

Stephen shrugged. "Joan hit the nail on the head. It seems most likely that once William Griffin was dead, it suddenly occurred to Galant that he could obtain Fox Hall if Red John died as well. William Griffin's death seems well planned, staged to look like the work of that gang to throw off suspicion. While Red John's murder seems more spontaneous. So I don't think Red John's death was part of Galant's original plan."

"Guesses are probably all we'll ever have," Harry said. "I'll bet Galant never turns up. Or —" he thrust a finger into the air at a sudden thought, "— he gets a pardon somehow."

"It wouldn't be the first time a murderer escaped justice by buying a pardon," Stephen said.

There was a knock at the door, an unusual event after dark. Sarah went to answer it. She returned with a boy of seven or eight.

"My lord," the boy stammered, his voice shaking. Tear tracks marred the dirt on his face. "Can you come? There's been a death."

The bottom dropped out of the evening, taking all the good feeling with it.

"What's happened, boy?" Stephen asked as kindly as he could manage, although he already knew the answer.

"It's, it's my mum," the boy cried. "Dad hit her and she fell down and hit her head. And now she's dead."

Stephen stood up. This was the only thing he could do. This is what people looked to him for. This is what his life had become, for good or ill.

"Show me the way."

Made in United States
Troutdale, OR
08/06/2024

21810701R00120